HAGGADAH

The Passover Story

This Haggadah is in memory of Haya bat Pinhas, Zal,
Mary Evelyn Kaplan (Naggar), (July 22, 1930–September 1, 2000).
Fully active, in the creative whirl of her life, Mary suddenly left us
on a beautiful autumn day, the first day of the Rosh Hodesh Ellul,
an exceptional moment when the doors of heaven are open with love
to accept the "return" of souls that have accomplished their mission on earth.
May her memory be a source of blessings for all of us!

Marc-Alain Ouaknin

© 2001 Assouline Publishing Inc.
Illustrations © 2001 Gérard Garouste

Assouline Publishing
601 West 26th Street
18th floor
New York, NY 10001

www.assouline.com

ISBN: 2 84323 253 8

Translated from the French by Jeffrey Green

Color separation: Gravor (Switzerland)
Printed by Pizzi (Italy)

HAGGADAH

The Passover Story

Gérard Garouste
Marc-Alain Ouaknin

ASSOULINE

THE PASSOVER FESTIVAL AND THE HAGGADAH

Pesach, the Jewish holiday of Passover, is one of the three pilgrimage festivals, along with Shavuoth ("the Feast of Weeks") and Sukkoth ("booths"). It falls on the fifteenth of Nissan, usually in the month of April, and lasts eight days (seven in Israel). The first and last two days are festival days, and the intervening four days are half-festivals, known in Hebrew as "Chol-Hamoed."

Pesach is both a religious and agricultural festival. It celebrates spring and the first barley harvest. It commemorates the Exodus of the Israelites from Egypt and the end of slavery. This commemoration is essential, because the Exodus from Egypt constitutes the founding event of the Jewish people. The Israelites had been enslaved for four hundred years when God, by the intermediary of Moses, aroused their desire for liberty.

Ten plagues were necessary to convince Pharaoh to allow the people to leave: blood, frogs, vermin, wild beasts, plague, boils, hail, locusts, darkness, and the slaying of the firstborn.

The word "Pesach" means "to pass over," because God passed over the houses of the Israelites during the tenth plague, sparing their firstborn. "Pesach" can also be read "Pe-Sach," meaning, "the mouth that speaks." Indeed, on Pesach it is an obligation to recount the story of the Exodus from Egypt and everything related to it. That is the meaning of the Haggadah, the Passover recitation.

THE MITZVOT (OBLIGATIONS) OF PESACH

The first obligation is the prohibition against consuming, possessing, or even seeing "chametz": any food containing leaven and, by extension, any food containing flour made from one of the five cereal grains: wheat, barley, oats, spelt, and rye, for these are the cereals that ferment.

The second obligation is to consume matzah—unleavened bread, the symbol of liberty but also the bread of affliction. It is the bread of liberty because the Israelites prepared it on the day of their departure from Egypt, and they did not have the time to let it rise. It is the bread of affliction because it was consumed by the Hebrew slaves in Egypt.

The third obligation is to celebrate the Seder or Passover meal. During the Seder, one tells the story of the Exodus from Egypt by reading the Haggadah.

Before coming to the Seder, many preparatory steps are necessary. Long before the holiday, one must begin to remove everything containing chametz from the home, the car, and the workplace. This thorough spring cleaning is still practiced today by both Jews and non-Jews.

On the evening of the thirteenth of Nissan, when night falls, "bedikat chametz," the search for anything leavened, is performed. By the light of a candle, one carefully looks for chametz in every corner of the house. The following morning, the chametz will be burned in the ceremony called "biur chametz." On the fourteenth of Nissan firstborn sons must fast in memory of the firstborn of Egypt. While a son is still a minor, his father fasts in his place.

On the evening of the fourteenth of Nissan, everyone gathers around the table, in the center of which stands the Seder Plate.

THE SEDER PLATE AND THE ORDER OF THE SEFIROT

The Passover meal is the quintessence of a family festival. It is called a "Seder," which means "order," because everything in that meal follows an extremely precise order, set out in a text that will be read like a program.

This text, distributed to every participant, is the Haggadah, the Passover story. This is the text that accompanies the Pesach ceremony.

The Haggadah is a text whose rhythm of songs and questions is truly a meditation on liberty.

The Haggadah is not only a book. It is also a practical guide that allows one to follow the course of the Seder ceremony.

A large platter, the Seder Plate, is placed in the center of the table, upon which are all the elements that will set the events of the evening in motion. The purpose of the evening is to make a theatrical presentation of the key memories of the Exodus from Egypt, to live them on the deepest level, and to make sure that one has the real feeling of living a moment of liberation.

The Seder is a ceremony where a central place is given to questioning, especially by children.

The questions concern unusual objects and unexpected ways of behaving: Why do we eat matzah (unleavened bread)? Why bitter herbs? Why must we eat and drink while leaning to the left?

To bring out the importance of questioning, many of the phrases of the Haggadah begin with the Hebrew word "Ma," which means "what." This applies particularly to the famous four questions that the children wait impatiently to chant out loud on the Seder night: "Ma nishtana halaila ha'zeh mikol haleilot," which is translated as, "In what way is this night different from all other nights?" This is one of the questions that the Haggadah seeks to answer throughout the evening.

A WELL ORDERED RITUAL

To understand the meaning of this evening, let us compare it to a ceremony that might be better known: the Japanese tea ceremony. People gather to drink tea according to a very precise and well organized ceremonial order. The way the water is heated, the number of tea leaves placed in the water, the order of the repast, the walks one takes before and after drinking the tea, the placement of the flower decorations and the plates in the room, the words that one says, and so on. Everything possesses precise significance that must be respected to make the ceremony succeed. Numerous works, guides, and manuals exist to allow the perfect execution of the tea ceremony, by which initiates correctly enter the "Way of the Tea," the Tchai-Do.

Similarly, the Seder is a ceremony by which the "initiates" enter the "Way of Liberty," by which they accomplish a passage: Passover.

This ceremony, whose form lies somewhere between theater and liturgy, is an apprenticeship in liberty and creativity through play, questions, mime, song, and an ensemble of symbols.

The Seder ceremony is very structured. It follows an exact plan of words and gestures that must be spoken and performed according to a certain order, which is the meaning of the Hebrew word "seder."

It is a paradox of liberty that it can only be attained within the framework of order, of rules, of words and symbols of extraordinary precision.

The rules of this ceremony were established and codified definitively in the Talmud around the second century C.E., at a time when Roman culture was dominant in the civilized world. This is an important fact, for it allows us to understand a certain number of gestures, attitudes, and culinary habits connected to that culture. Once the Seder was codified, it was never changed, and, as astonishing as this may appear, Jews today, once a year, behave in a way connected with second century Roman civilization.

The Passover evening recital progresses through a fourteen-stage structure.

The Seder ceremony takes place around a table in the center of which is enthroned a large platter, the Seder Plate, and the symbolic foods of the ceremony are arranged on that dish.

THE SEDER PLATE

The various symbolic elements that will be shown, tasted, and commented upon during the Passover evening are arranged on a large plate.

The Seder Plate contains all the symbols of the holiday. On it are a roasted bone, a hard-boiled egg, a cup of salt water, a fruit compote called "charoset," bitter herbs (maror—generally horseradish, but romaine lettuce, radish, or endive can also be used), a leafy vegetable (karpas), and, in the center of the platter, three pieces of unleavened bread. The placement of these different elements varies according to different traditions.

1 The roasted bone recalls the sacrifice of the paschal lamb on the night of the Exodus from Egypt, the animal whose blood was used to mark the doors of Jewish homes so they would be spared the death of their firstborn (see the account of this event in Exodus XII and following chapters). The sacrifice of the lamb was the first sign of liberty for the Israelites, because the lamb was an Egyptian god. To dare to sacrifice a god represented, for a people of slaves, a gesture of enormous courage and absolute confidence.

2 The hard-boiled egg recalls the sacrifice that was brought on every pilgrimage festival, known as "Korban Chagiga." It is also a symbol of mourning that recalls the destruction of the Temple in Jerusalem.

3   The charoset is a paste resembling mortar made of ground apples and nuts, cinnamon, red wine, and ginger, or else made from date paste, nuts, and apples. It is meant to recall the bricks that the Israelites had to make by themselves to construct cities and monuments for the Pharaoh.

4   The maror—the bitter herbs—may be romaine lettuce, endive, radish, black radish, or horseradish, depending on the tradition. It recalls the bitterness of slavery, because the Egyptians were not satisfied merely with making the Israelites work very hard, but they persecuted them, tormented them physically by degrading their bodily integrity and psychologically by placing them in situations where they themselves had to deliver their children to certain death.

5   The karpas—a leafy vegetable, like parsley or celery–, recalls the leaves that were used to sprinkle the doors of the Israelites with blood from the paschal lamb.

6   The salt water in the cup recalls the tears and sweat shed by the Israelites enslaved in Egypt.

7   The three matzot symbolize the three patriarchs—Abraham, Isaac, and Jacob—or the three categories of Jews—Cohen, Levi, and Israel.

THE FOUR CUPS OF WINE

During the Seder, four cups of wine are drunk that evoke the words for liberty used in the Bible to tell the story of the Exodus from Egypt. Today, there is a custom of drinking five cups of wine.

In order to give further emphasis to the importance of liberation and liberty, the four cups must be drunk while leaning to the left, because at the time when the Seder was instituted (the Roman period), only free men could eat while reclining on sofas.

The end of the Seder is marked by eating the afikoman, a small piece of matzah that is hidden and then found again. The word "afikoman" comes from the Greek and means "dessert," but the Hasidic masters proposed another derivation for the word from the Aramaic, reading it as "Afiku-man," meaning "make the question come out!" We shall explain this in our commentary.

The Seder concludes with songs, the most famous of which is about "the kid that my father bought for two zuzim."

Beginning with the second night of Pesach, one counts, evening after evening, the forty-nine days leading to the holiday of Shavuoth (weeks), a period called the "counting of the Omer."

THE HAGGADAH ILLUSTRATED BY GÉRARD GAROUSTE

Of all the texts in the Jewish tradition, it is the Haggadah that, generation after generation, has most consistently received the homage of artists, who have viewed it as an honor and almost a duty to place their talent in the service of this text of liberty. Gérard Garouste, one of France's leading contemporary painters, for his pleasure and for ours, has agreed to enter into dialogue with the text of the Haggadah. He has not created an illustration, but a veritable interpretation. Garouste reads, writes, and has mastered the Hebrew language. Thus, he has tried and certainly succeeded *in entering the depths of this work and deciphering its enigmas on the basis of the original text.*

But instead of a simple transposition of word to image, Garouste, through the grammar of his universe, offers a commentary that becomes an integral part of the Haggadah, on the same footing as a traditional commentary. The reader of this Haggadah will be able both to inquire into the meaning of the images and seek their internal coherence, and also to study the interplay between the Hebrew text and the commentaries we have added. Garouste has not only read the Haggadah, he has studied it, and he has descended into the mysteries of the square letters to bring out the sparks of transcendence and sacred light, the sparks that dwell there permanently. Garouste is a serious painter. He knows how to play not only with light and its absence but also with the eye-to-come of the reader-viewer. It also means that the reader-viewer of these often astonishing images must not simply look at them, but also discover the hidden question to which each image aspires to be an answer and a dialogue with tradition.

For our part, we have tried to be as clear as possible in presenting the symbolism of the ensemble of gestures that preside over the proper unfolding of the Passover evening, and also in offering a reflection that underlines the different articulations of that evening, notably the fourteen parts of this course of initiation.

May the viewers and readers in their turn, in this dialogue of images and words, feel free to invent their own liberty.

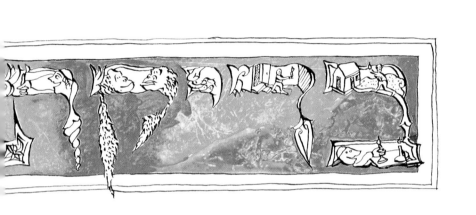

BEDIKAT CHAMETZ

בְּדִיקַת חָמֵץ

BEDIKAT CHAMETZ

searching for chametz

ON THE EVENING BEFORE PESACH, ONE MUST SEARCH FOR CHAMETZ THROUGHOUT THE HOUSE. BEFORE BEGINNING THE SEARCH FOR CHAMETZ ONE SHOULD WASH HIS HANDS AND RECITE THE FOLLOWING BLESSING WITH JOY:

בָּרוּךְ אַתָּה יְיָ אֱלֹהֵינוּ מֶלֶךְ
הָעוֹלָם אֲשֶׁר קִדְּשָׁנוּ בְּמִצוֹתָיו
וְצִוָּנוּ עַל בִּעוּר חָמֵץ׃

**Blessed are You, God,
King of the universe,
Who has made us holy
with His mitzvot,
and commanded us
to remove chametz.**

UPON COMPLETION, THE CHAMETZ IS SET ASIDE AND THE FOLLOWING DECLARATION IS THEN SAID:

כָּל־חֲמִירָא וַחֲמִיעָה דְּאִכָּא
בִרְשׁוּתִי דְּלָא חֲמִתֵּהּ וּדְלָא
בִעַרְתֵּהּ לִבָּטֵל וְלֶהֱוֵי כְּעַפְרָא
דְאַרְעָא׃

**Any chametz in my possession
which I did not see,
remove, or know about,
shall be nullified
and become ownerless
as the dust of the earth.**

ON THE MORNING OF THE 14TH DAY OF NISSAN, THE EVE OF PESACH, ONE MUST DISPOSE OF ALL CHAMETZ IN HIS POSSESSION. ONE THEN BURNS THE CHAMETZ. THE FOLLOWING DECLARATION IS TO BE MADE AFTER BURNING THE CHAMETZ.

כָּל־חֲמִירָא וַחֲמִיעָה דְּאִכָּא
בִרְשׁוּתִי דַּחֲזִתֵּהּ וּדְלָא חֲמִתֵּהּ
דְּבִעַרְתֵּהּ וּדְלָא בִעַרְתֵּהּ לִבְטִיל
וְלֶהֱוֵי כְּעַפְרָא דְאַרְעָא׃

**Any chametz in my possession
which I did or did not see,
which I did or did not destroy
shall be nullified
and become ownerless
as the dust of the earth.**

Blessed are You,
God, King of the universe,
Who has made us holy
with His mitzvot, and commanded
us to keep the mitzvah of Eruv.
With this Eruv, we shall be
permitted to bake, cook, roast,
keep food warm, kindle a flame,
and do all the necessary
preparations for Shabbat
on the festival; we and all Jews
who live in this city.

בָּרוּךְ אַתָּה יְיָ אֱלֹהֵינוּ מֶלֶךְ
הָעוֹלָם אֲשֶׁר קִדְּשָׁנוּ בְּמִצְוֹתָיו
וְצִוָּנוּ עַל מִצְוַת עֵרוּב:
בְּדֵין עֵרוּבָא יְהֵא שְׁרֵא לָנָא
לְמֵיפָא וּלְבַשְׁלָא וּלְאַטְמָנָא
וּלְאַדְלָקָא שְׁרָגָא וּלְמֶעְבַּד כָּל-
צָרְכָנָא מִיּוֹמָא טָבָא לְשַׁבַּתָּא.
לָנוּ וּלְכָל-הַדָּרִים בְּעִיר הַזֹּאת:

 קַדֵּשׁ

Kadesh

 וּרְחַץ

Urchatz

 כַּרְפַּס

Karpas

 יַחַץ

Yachatz

 מַגִּיד

Maggid

 רָחְצָה

Rachatzah

 מוֹצִיא מַצָּה

Motzi-Matzah

מָרוֹר
Maror

כּוֹרֵך
Korech

שֻׁלְחָן עוֹרֵך
Shulchan Orech

צָפוּן
Tzafun

בָּרֵך
Barech

הַלֵּל
Hallel

נִרְצָה
Nirtzah

Part One

KADESH

KADESH

drinking the first cup of wine

THE FIRST CUP OF WINE IS FILLED.
ON FRIDAY EVENING, BEGIN HERE:

וַיְהִי עֶרֶב וַיְהִי בֹקֶר יוֹם הַשִּׁשִּׁי: וַיְכֻלּוּ הַשָּׁמַיִם וְהָאָרֶץ
וְכָל־צְבָאָם: וַיְכַל אֱלֹהִים בַּיּוֹם הַשְּׁבִיעִי מְלַאכְתּוֹ אֲשֶׁר
עָשָׂה וַיִּשְׁבֹּת בַּיּוֹם הַשְּׁבִיעִי מִכָּל־מְלַאכְתּוֹ אֲשֶׁר עָשָׂה:
וַיְבָרֶךְ אֱלֹהִים אֶת־יוֹם הַשְּׁבִיעִי וַיְקַדֵּשׁ אֹתוֹ כִּי בוֹ שָׁבַת
מִכָּל־מְלַאכְתּוֹ, אֲשֶׁר בָּרָא אֱלֹהִים לַעֲשׂוֹת:

And it was evening and it was morning.
The Sixth Day. The heavens and the earth were finished, and all that was in them.
On the Seventh Day God completed His work, that which He had done,
and He abstained on the Seventh Day from all His work which He had done.
God blessed the Seventh Day and sanctified it, because on it
He abstained from all His work which God created to make (Genesis 1:31-2:3).

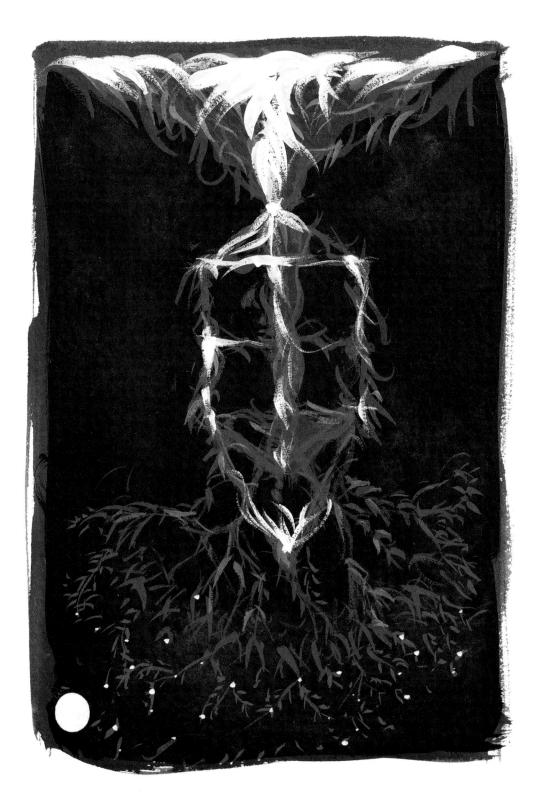

סַבְרִי מָרָנָן וְרַבָּנָן וְרַבּוֹתַי:
בָּרוּךְ אַתָּה יְיָ אֱלֹהֵינוּ מֶלֶךְ הָעוֹלָם בּוֹרֵא
פְּרִי הַגָּפֶן:

בָּרוּךְ אַתָּה יְיָ אֱלֹהֵינוּ מֶלֶךְ הָעוֹלָם, אֲשֶׁר בָּחַר בָּנוּ
מִכָּל־עָם, וְרוֹמְמָנוּ מִכָּל־לָשׁוֹן, וְקִדְּשָׁנוּ בְּמִצְוֹתָיו. וַתִּתֶּן־לָנוּ
יְיָ אֱלֹהֵינוּ בְּאַהֲבָה (שַׁבָּתוֹת לִמְנוּחָה וּ)מוֹעֲדִים לְשִׂמְחָה
חַגִּים וּזְמַנִּים לְשָׂשׂוֹן אֶת־יוֹם (הַשַּׁבָּת הַזֶּה וְאֶת־יוֹם) חַג
הַמַּצּוֹת הַזֶּה. זְמַן חֵרוּתֵנוּ (בְּאַהֲבָה) מִקְרָא קֹדֶשׁ,
זֵכֶר לִיצִיאַת מִצְרָיִם. כִּי בָנוּ בָחַרְתָּ וְאוֹתָנוּ קִדַּשְׁתָּ
מִכָּל־הָעַמִּים.

Blessed are You, God,
King of the universe,
Who creates
the fruit of the vine.

Blessed are You, God,
King of the universe,
Who has chosen us
from all the nations,
exalted us above
all languages,
and made us holy
with His mitzvot.
You, our God, have
given us, with love,
(Sabbaths for rest,)
special times for
gladness, festivals and
seasons for joy,

(וְשַׁבָּת) וּמוֹעֲדֵי קָדְשֶׁךָ (בְּאַהֲבָה וּבְרָצוֹן) בְּשִׂמְחָה
וּבְשָׂשׂוֹן הִנְחַלְתָּנוּ. בָּרוּךְ אַתָּה יְיָ מְקַדֵּשׁ
(הַשַּׁבָּת וְ)יִשְׂרָאֵל וְהַזְּמַנִּים:

(this Sabbath and) this Festival
of matzot, the season
of our freedom, (in love,)
a holy convocation, recalling
the Exodus from Egypt.
For You have chosen and
sanctified us above all peoples,
(and the Sabbath) and
Your holy festivals (in love and
favor), in gladness and joy
You have granted us.
Blessed are You, God,
Who sanctifies (the Sabbath,)
Israel and the Festivals.

ON SATURDAY NIGHT, ADD
THE FOLLOWING TWO BLESSINGS

Blessed are You, God,
King of the universe,
Who creates the lights of fire.

בָּרוּךְ אַתָּה יְיָ אֱלֹהֵינוּ מֶלֶךְ
הָעוֹלָם בּוֹרֵא מְאוֹרֵי הָאֵשׁ:

Blessed are You, God,
King of the universe,
Who distinguishes between
holy and mundane, between
light and darkness, between
Israel and the nations, between
the Seventh Day and the six days
of work; between the holiness
of Shabbat and the holiness
of a Festival You have
distinguished and have sanctified
Shabbat above the six days of
work. You distinguished and
sanctified Your nation, Israel,
with Your holiness. Blessed are
You, God, Who distinguishes
between [one] holiness
and [another] holiness.

בָּרוּךְ אַתָּה יְיָ אֱלֹהֵינוּ מֶלֶךְ
הָעוֹלָם הַמַּבְדִּיל בֵּין קֹדֶשׁ לְחֹל
בֵּין אוֹר לְחֹשֶׁךְ בֵּין יִשְׂרָאֵל
לָעַמִּים בֵּין יוֹם הַשְּׁבִיעִי לְשֵׁשֶׁת
יְמֵי הַמַּעֲשֶׂה. בֵּין קְדֻשַּׁת שַׁבָּת
לִקְדֻשַּׁת יוֹם טוֹב הִבְדַּלְתָּ וְאֶת־
יוֹם הַשְּׁבִיעִי מִשֵּׁשֶׁת יְמֵי
הַמַּעֲשֶׂה קִדַּשְׁתָּ. הִבְדַּלְתָּ וְקִדַּשְׁתָּ
אֶת־עַמְּךָ יִשְׂרָאֵל בִּקְדֻשָּׁתֶךָ.
בָּרוּךְ אַתָּה יְיָ הַמַּבְדִּיל בֵּין קֹדֶשׁ
לְקֹדֶשׁ:

ON ALL NIGHTS CONCLUDE HERE.

Blessed are You, God,
King of the universe,
Who has kept us alive,
sustained us, and
brought us to this season.

בָּרוּךְ אַתָּה יְיָ אֱלֹהֵינוּ מֶלֶךְ
הָעוֹלָם שֶׁהֶחֱיָנוּ וְקִיְּמָנוּ וְהִגִּיעָנוּ
לַזְּמַן הַזֶּה:

DRINK THE WINE WHILE RECLINING
TO THE LEFT SIDE. MORE THAN
HALF THE CUP SHOULD BE DRUNK.

KADESH

drinking the first cup of wine

THE SANCTIFICATION

The first part of the Seder is the recitation of the kiddush or "sanctification." This blessing is recited over a glass of wine, the first of the four cups of wine that everyone is obliged to drink during the Seder night to remind us of the four expressions that the Torah uses for the deliverance from Egypt:

I will bring you out ...

I will deliver you ...

I will save you ...

I will take you ...

This first and relatively short part of the ceremony begins the Seder evening with the sanctification of the day, or the "kiddush." "Kadesh" comes from the same root as "kadosh," meaning "holy." This sanctification is not specific to the Pesach holiday. It inaugurates all the Jewish holidays and every Shabbat, the seventh day of the week.

The kiddush is the sanctification of time.

In Hebrew, that which is sanctified is separated. A famous saying by the great Bible commentator Rashi (Rabbi Shlomo Yitzchaki) reads: "ein kiddush ela bimkom havdala"—"there is no sanctification except where there is separation." That which is sanctified is set apart; it is not like other things; it has a particular meaning of its own, unique. Sacred time is thus a time sanctified by consciousness of its particularity. It is not like all the other moments that follow upon one another and resemble one another. Thus it is an event!

The sanctification of time is the transformation of time into an Event.

The sanctification of time is a challenge that people give to themselves at the inauguration of every holiday, a challenge that is the very essence of the holiday, of Passover and all the others: to see to it that something extraordinary happens.

The first part of the evening is the kadesh, because it is the key to the meaning of the evening: to open oneself to the Event. The thirteen other parts of the Passover ceremony are merely commentaries on the themes and variations upon this fundamental, even foundational experience!

The Haggadah is a story. The Hebrew root of the word is "nagod," which means "to oppose," to go against that which exists in the banality of the repetition of the day-to-day.

The Haggadah is the story of the Exodus from Egypt. Not only from a physical Egypt, but also and above all from the Egypt of banality of the day-to-day, where things lose their taste and meaning in their repetitions. In its way, the Haggadah explores the organized and organizing forces that work toward uniformity in a given society. Uniformity of thought, of feeling, and of being, of which the banal is the ultimate expression.

The essential problem of the banal is the disappearance of the imaginary and of the dream, and because of that, the disappearance of projection toward somewhere else, toward another scene, a projection that is the very movement of a person's humanity.

To be is not merely "to be," but to be able to be differently. That is the true meaning of liberty!

The search for that space between being and being able to be, between saying and being able to say, between reality and dream is at the center of the Passover story, and it is to that search that we devote this book.

In the text of the kiddush, the first part of the Seder, we recall that God brought us out of Egypt. That formula is a reminder of the first of the Ten Commandments, which says, "I am the Eternal One, your God, who brought you out of the land of Egypt, out of the house of bondage..." The meaning of the kiddush is the same as that of the first of the Ten Commandments, which proposes an ensemble of processes that allow one to free oneself from the institutionalized forms of experience, to invent new forms of life. A person's different actions must try to invent new forms of experience that are never assigned: to exit from banality.

Such an ethic is not an abstract duty, but an option in life. The person who hears the First Commandment, who agrees to leave Egypt, who understands that if there is a God, He is a God of liberation, is a person of "chiddush," of novelty.

Part Two

URCHATZ

URCHATZ

washing and purifying the hands

The second part of the Seder is called urchatz—meaning "and one washes"—washing of the hands.

This is a small ritual ceremony, which for each participant consists of pouring water on their hands from a small vessel called a "keli" or "natla" and reserved for that purpose.

There are several ways of pouring the water. Generally one first pours water three times on the right hand and then three times on the left.

Others alternate between the right and left hands, pouring water three times on each hand.

No blessing is recited. In some families only the leader of the Seder washes his hands.

The Talmud teaches that the meal is a symbolic way of accomplishing the sacrificial cult of the Temple: "shulchan do'meh la'mizbe'ach" or "the table is similar to the altar."

Thus, before eating bread or food soaked in a liquid, it is customary to purify one's hands to emphasize the ritual aspect of the meal. The foods that the priests ate in the Temple in Jerusalem were pure.

Below, in the explanations of the washing of hands before consuming matzah, we discuss the meaning of the concept of purity.

Like the priests, when we sit at the table, we begin by purifying our hands, to emphasize that eating food is far more than a simple nutritive activity. The ritual, not merely hygienic washing of the hands creates a symbolic break, and we enter into another space and time, that of the sacred and of ritual. It is the construction of another setting, the elsewhere of memory and hope. Thus a new world opens!

The play of coming and going between this world and the other one, a play of projections of dreams and interpretations, of transcendence and immanence, of coming and going between banality and creativity, between the profane and the sacred—all of this play may begin.

The "purification" of the hands is thus a way of entering the play of the festival, of accepting the rules of the game that constitute this festive night.

Part Three

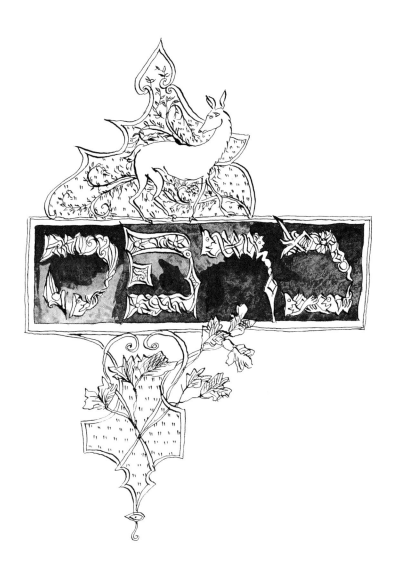

KARPASS

KARPAS

dipping vegetables in salt water

EVERYONE TAKES A SMALL PIECE OF A VEGETABLE (CUCUMBER, PARSLEY, POTATO, ETC.)
OTHER THAN MAROR, DIPS IT INTO SALT WATER, AND RECITES THE FOLLOWING
BLESSING (ONE SHOULD BEAR IN MIND THAT
THE BLESSING ALSO APPLIES TO THE MAROR AND TO THE KORECH):

Blessed are You, God,
King of the universe,
Who creates the fruit of the earth.

EAT THE KARPAS WITHOUT RECLINING.

KARPAS

dipping vegetables in salt water

We are now at the beginning of this course of initiation, this "initiatory play," as one might say.

This third part of the Seder consists in taking a piece of celery, chervil, lettuce, endive, or another vegetable that grows on the ground, and dipping it in salt water or vinegar. Usually the head of the family distributes a branch of celery to each participant. Everyone present then recites the benediction, "borai pri haadama"—"who creates the fruit of the earth"—which is recited when eating foods coming from the earth.

The purpose of this ritual is, first of all, to awaken the curiosity of the children and oblige them to ask questions. When they ask, "Why this ritual?" adults will answer: "Vegetables dipped in salt water remind us of the meager meals eaten by our ancestors when they were slaves in Egypt, drenched in sweat and tears."

Some people offer the following commentary: During the Exodus from Egypt, God said to the Children of Israel, "And you shall take a bunch of hyssop and dip it in the blood that is in the basin, and touch the lintel and the two door posts with the blood that is in the basin. And none of you shall go out at the door of house until the morning. For the Lord will pass through to smite Egypt; and when He sees the blood that is on the lintel and on the two door posts, the Lord will pass over the door, and will not permit the destroyer to come into your houses to smite you. And you shall observe this thing for an ordinance to you and to your sons forever.... And it shall come to pass, when your children say to you, 'What is this service to you?' you shall say, 'it is a paschal sacrifice to the Lord, who passed over the houses of the children of Israel in Egypt and saved our houses.'" The tradition of dipping a sprig of a vegetable in salt water, karpas, reminds us of the branch of hyssop dipped in blood to mark the outlines of the doors of the Israelites' houses in Egypt. One may elaborate upon the karpas ritual in the following way: using a sprig of celery, sprinkle the outlines of the door of the house to place it "under protection."

The karpas would thus be related to the rite of the "mezuza," the parchment one attaches to all the doors of a house, also for protection. Moreover, the name of God, "ShaDaY," is written on the mezuza, and this name is an acronym of the words, "Shomer Daltot Yisrael," the guardian of the doors of Israel.

According to the Bible, the performance of this ritual arouses the curiosity of the children who are watching, so they ask questions about the meaning of this tradition. The answer explains the name of the holiday, Pesach, "He passed over us."

If karpas is essentially the ritual of marking a door, it also provides a chance to imagine. Karpas is one of the primary conditions of liberation: setting the imagination in motion. But, as Bachelard says:

"Imagination is not only, as its etymology suggests, the faculty of forming images of reality; it is the faculty of forming images that go beyond reality, that sing reality. It is a faculty of superhumanity. A person is a person in proportion to his being superhuman. One must define a person by the ensemble of tendencies that drive him to go beyond the human condition. ...Imagination invents more than things and dramas. It invents a new life. It invents a new spirit. It opens eyes that have new types of vision." (Translated from Gaston Bachelard, L'Eau et les rêves, pp. 23-24).

KARPAS: A UNIQUE WORD

When one wishes to understand the meaning of a word, one must see in what context it first appears in the Bible. Then one finds the most essential use of the word whose later appearances in the text are merely themes and variations. That is the rule of first occurrence. But when a word appears only once, it is designated by the Greek term "hapax legomenon."

"Karpas" is such a word. It appears just once in the Bible, in the Book of Esther (1:6). The passage where it appears describes the various rich textiles that King Ahasuerus displayed

*in order to show his wealth during the celebrations that he held in Shushan during
the third year of his reign. According to Solomon Mandelkern, "karpas" is a Persian
word designating a sumptuous cloth, a veil of wool and white linen. Karpas is thus
connected with the Book of Esther. Esther is also a name derived from the Persian,
"Astarte." In Hebrew, it is understood as "concealment" (Talmud, Hulin 139b),
because in Hebrew "aster" means "I will conceal." (On the link between Purim and
Pesach, see Rabbi Nachman of Bratslav,* Likutei Moharan *II, 74.)*

   *This invitation to pass from the text of the Haggadah to that of the Book
of Esther by this intertextual play is in itself the first commentary on karpas.*

   *Karpas is liberation by the movement of opening that produces intertextuality. Intertextuality
is a doorway onto another context and another imaginary realm. This "passage" from one text
to another is the very meaning of the name "Hebrew" (ivri), which comes from the root, "la'avor,"
"to pass." The Hebrew is thus a "passer." For the Hebrew, to exist is to become. He is in a constant
becoming, a be-coming that is a future, a to-coming. The Hebrew person is messianic, if messianism
is not only the certitude of the arrival of someone who alters history, but a way of being for every
person in his inscription within the becoming of time. Hebrew, the language of passage, is set in
motion in the play of intertextuality, this play of coming and going between two texts, and by the
existence of a word in common, karpas.*

   *Hebrew is not "the Hebrew language," the sum of words and linguistic operations that one
can find in a dictionary or grammar book, but it is the functioning of the language as a bridge
and passage from one cultural universe to another. Hebrew is the passage from one bank of a river
to another.*

   *In Hebrew, the word for "river bank" is "safa," which also means "language." Passing from
one bank to another is to pass from one language to another, translating into an action the fact
that karpas is a Persian word.*

   *Hebrew is always a language that contains languages. It is, precisely, the dynamic and
dialectic movement between two languages.*

   Another word for "river bank" is "gada." The direction of movement toward a bank, the opposite bank, can be called "haggadah." Reading the Haggadah on Pesach is constantly to remember.

Two Talmudic Sages, Rabbi Chiya Rabba and Rabbi Shimon ben Halafta, discuss whether one should consider the karpas-veil as the curtain of a theater or as the sail of a boat.

Karpas is a sail, a theater curtain that hides and unveils... Here we enter fully into a dialectic between the visible and the invisible, of presence and absence, which will unfold throughout the Pesach night....

The sail allows the boat to move forward thanks to wind power. That power is, however, invisible.

Part Four

YACHATZ

YACHATZ

breaking the matzah in two

THE MIDDLE MATZAH IS BROKEN INTO TWO UNEQUAL PARTS. THE SMALLER PART IS REPLACED
BETWEEN THE TWO WHOLE MATZOT, AND THE LARGER PART IS PUT AWAY FOR LATER USE
AS THE AFIKOMAN. THERE IS A CUSTOM THAT CHILDREN TRY TO "STEAL" THE AFIKOMAN,
AND THEN TRY TO RANSOM IT WHEN THE TIME COMES FOR IT TO BE EATEN.
(THE HOST SHOULD BE AWARE THAT IF THE RANSOM IS HIGH, ONE IS PERMITTED TO USE
ANOTHER PIECE OF MATZAH, JUST AS IN THE CASE IF THE AFIKOMAN WAS LOST.)

DEPARTURE ON A VOYAGE

*The head of the family takes the middle matzah and divides it in two. This ordinary gesture
has great symbolic weight. This gesture is, first of all, an invitation for the poor and the stranger
to share the bread and the memory. This breaking is also in memory of crossing the Red Sea,
which was divided in two to allow the passage of the Israelites as they left Egypt. In some families,
it is customary to wrap the broken matzah in a napkin, which the head of the family places on
his shoulder. He walks toward the door, and the participants in the Seder ask him: "Where are you
coming from? And where are you going?" He answers: "I come from a certain place and I am
going to Jerusalem." Every participant then does the same thing.*

*Among the Sephardim, it is customary for the head of the family to pass the plate over the head
of every guest and speak the phrase: "Bivehilu yatzanu mi'mitzrayim"—"we hurriedly left Egypt."*

RITUAL AND PLAY

*The large piece of the matzah, which one keeps for the end of the meal, has the name of
"afikoman," a word of Greek derivation that means "dessert." One tradition is to break the matzah
in the form of the Hebrew letter dalet, which means "door" and has the numerical value of four.
This is the door that we open at the start of the Seder to invite the stranger in, that we open at
the end of the meal to greet the prophet Elijah, the door that we open in our spirit to penetrate
the world of imagination and to leave behind banality. And it is the door that we open to play
here, that we open to a new definition of human beings as creatures capable of play.*

*Indeed, Yachatz is the signal given for the beginning of a great game of hide and seek that will
occupy all of the evening's participants. There are two traditions for the game. In one, the head of*

EXODUS 12:34

the family or some other adult takes the afikoman and hides it. The children then look for it all throughout the meal. The one who finds the afikoman will give it to the master of the house, then bargain for a present of his or her choice. In the other tradition, the children hide the matzah, and the parents look for it.

This is the game of hide and seek that has inaugurated every Pesach festival. Indeed, on the fourteenth of Nissan, the eve of Pesach, after the meticulous Passover cleaning, when there is not a single piece of bread or anything associated with bread in the house, the children hide ten little pieces of bread, wrapped in paper so that they won't crumble. Then the parents amuse themselves by looking for those pieces of bread scattered throughout the house. The following morning, the pieces of bread will be burned. The search for the pieces of bread is called "bedikat chametz" (the search for chametz), and the ritual of burning them is called "biur chametz" (the eradication or disappearance of chametz). Here, too, there is an opposite tradition, in which the parents hide the pieces of bread and the children look for them.

What is the meaning of this play?

Why play?

And why play hide and seek?

I believe that here the Haggadah allows us to discover an essential dimension of humanity. A human being is not defined, as Descartes thought, by his or her capacity to think ("I think, therefore I am"). A human being is not "homo cogitans," but rather "homo ludens."

Here, play enters the heart of the Seder, an "order" of things that are organized in a certain way.

The order is the ceremony, the gestures that recur according to a set rhythm and that construct the limits of space and mark the stages of the calendar.

There is a double relation of correspondence and opposition between ritual and play: both are linked to time and space, but by an inverse relationship. Ritual establishes and creates structure; play, by contrast, changes and destroys structure. More precisely, one may say that time and space exist as a result of an intriguing combination of ritual and play. As Levi-Strauss says, "Whereas ritual transforms events into structures, play transform structures into events."

Structure is synchronic (everything takes place at the same time), whereas play is open to the diachronic, to the event that produces the dispersion of moments, the emergence of something completely new.

Ritual is a force of cohesion that tends to transform the diachronic into the synchronic: separate events are organized into the same story, the same account, the same narrative and gestural structure.

Play, by contrast, is a force of dispersion that seeks to transform synchronicity into diachronicity. But ritual and play cannot easily be separated. Every game partakes of ritual, and every ritual partakes of play.

What results from these two tendencies, between structuring and dispersal, is History, which is to say, human time!

Every society possesses a history. There is no society without a history. I do not think that the distinction made by Levi-Strauss between "warm societies" and "cold societies" has become outmoded. "Cold" societies are those in which the sphere of ritual tends to develop at the expense of the sphere of play. "Warm" societies are those where the sphere of play tends to develop at the expense of the ritual sphere.

Pesach and the Seder night reestablish the equilibrium between play and ritual, between structure and event—in a word, human time.

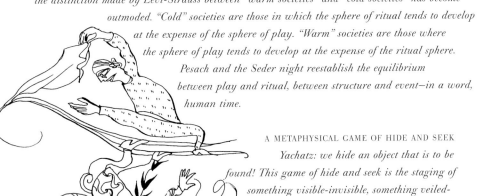

A METAPHYSICAL GAME OF HIDE AND SEEK

Yachatz: we hide an object that is to be found! This game of hide and seek is the staging of something visible-invisible, something veiled-unveiled that is connected to the idea we mentioned in the commentary on karpas.

Nevertheless, we think that the implications of this game have an essential metaphysical and *psychological bearing. We must try to understand how and why this play is born. Reading a well-known text by Freud can give us an orientation for understanding.*

In Beyond the Pleasure Principle, *Freud describes the play of his young son, one and a half years old, who amused himself at first by taking every object within reach and throwing it out of his bed, crying out "Oh-oh-oh!" Then he threw a reel attached to a cord, making it disappear and then reappear, reinforcing his play by crying "Oh-oh-oh!" when he threw it and "Ah-ah-ah!" when the object reappeared.*

Freud interpreted this game and the sounds accompanying it in the following manner. "Oh" and "Ah" are childish forms of the German words "fort" ("away") and "da" ("here"), in other words, "gone" and "come back." There is no doubt, according to P. Fédida, in L'absence *(translated from* L'absence, *Gallimard, 1978), that this play with the reel, of which numerous variants could be written, concerns an effort at symbolic mastery of absence and its object. With play, the child actively controls the disappearance and reappearance of its mother. Its anguish at seeing the mother disappear is overcome by the certitude of seeing her reappear, just as he knows, through the repetitive power of the game, that the reel will reappear.*

This game is connected to separation—to the child's capacity to separate itself from the mother's body.

Winnicot explains in L'absence *by P. Fédida (Gallimard, 1978) that the time of weaning is when the child becomes capable of playing at dropping objects. This is the discovery of the object through play; the play consists in opening the hand, losing one's grip. The object is thus constituted as signifying separation, abandonment, or loss. The child must be able to open its hand to allow the object to be. One could almost say to liberate the object.*

But why discuss mothers, separation anxiety and weaning in the context of the Seder?

The Exodus from Egypt is like a birth and the Israelites in the desert are like a young child still tied to its symbolic mother: the land of Egypt.

At first, the Bible tells us that the Israelites were not yet ready for weaning. Indeed, when they see Moses disappear, when he climbs to the top of Mount Sinai to receive the Torah, the Israelites create a golden calf, an object designed to overcome the anxiety of the disappearance of the mother and of the one who represented her: Moses.

Moses himself taught us how to attain liberty and autonomy through a famous gesture:

throwing down the tablets of the law. It is not so much
their shattering that is important as the fact of throwing
them down, of opening the hands, of letting the object
go and liberating it. The body of the mother and
child, who formed a symbiotic unity, opens up
to duality. This is also one of the important
meanings of the breaking and covering of Yachatz,
of the large and small piece of matzah, the
mother and the child.

Thus the act of hiding the large
piece of matzah is equivalent to
making the mother's body
disappear, and to showing
mastery of the possibility of
her return. The play of the
afikoman on the Seder night
is a way of acting out the
question of the presence
or absence of God
in history, and the
disposition to confront
oneself with that question
which is so essential.

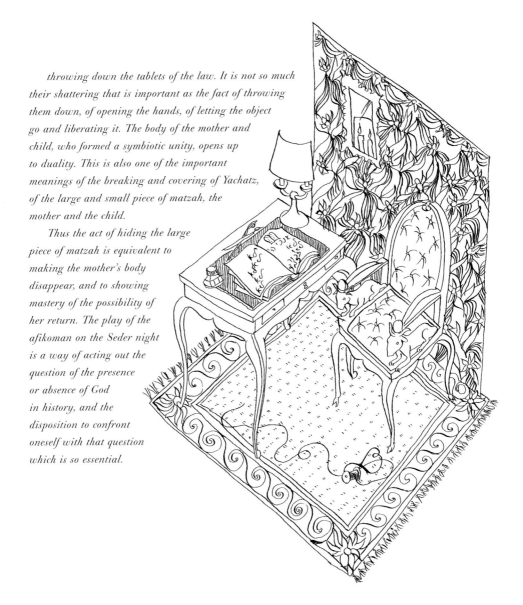

Part Five

MAGGID

מַגִּיד

MAGGID

telling the story of the Exodus from Egypt

THROUGHOUT THE EVENING, WHEN RECITING THE HAGGADAH,

THE MATZOT SHOULD BE UNCOVERED. HOWEVER, WHENEVER THE CUPS OF WINE

IS LIFTED OR HELD, THE MATZOT SHOULD BE COVERED.

הָא לַחְמָא עַנְיָא דִי אֲכָלוּ אַבְהָתָנָא בְּאַרְעָא דְמִצְרָיִם. כָּל
דְּכְפִין יֵיתֵי וְיֵכוֹל, כָּל דְּצְרִיךְ יֵיתֵי וְיִפְסַח. הָשַׁתָּא הָכָא.
לְשָׁנָה הַבָּאָה בְּאַרְעָא דְיִשְׂרָאֵל. הָשַׁתָּא עַבְדֵי. לְשָׁנָה
הַבָּאָה בְּנֵי חוֹרִין:

This is the bread of affliction that our fathers ate in the land of Egypt.
All who are hungry, come and eat!
All in need, come and join in celebrating Pesach!
This year we are here, next year we will be in the land of Israel!
This year we are slaves, next year we will be free men!

AT NIGHT

Why is this night different
from all other nights?

[Why is it] that on all nights
we may eat either chametz
or matzah, and on this night
we may eat only matzah?

[Why is it] that on all other
nights we may eat any kind
of vegetables, and on this night
we may eat only maror?

[Why is it] that on all other
nights we are not required
to dip our foods even once,
and on this night we are
required to do so twice?

[Why is it] that on all other
nights we may eat either
sitting or reclining, and on this
night we must recline?

מַה נִּשְׁתַּנָּה הַלַּיְלָה הַזֶּה מִכָּל
הַלֵּילוֹת.
שֶׁבְּכָל הַלֵּילוֹת אָנוּ אוֹכְלִין
חָמֵץ וּמַצָּה. הַלַּיְלָה הַזֶּה
כֻּלּוֹ מַצָּה:
שֶׁבְּכָל־הַלֵּילוֹת אָנוּ אוֹכְלִין
שְׁאָר יְרָקוֹת הַלַּיְלָה הַזֶּה מָרוֹר:
שֶׁבְּכָל־הַלֵּילוֹת אֵין אָנוּ
מַטְבִּילִין אֲפִילוּ פַּעַם אֶחָת.
הַלַּיְלָה הַזֶּה שְׁתֵּי פְעָמִים:
שֶׁבְּכָל־הַלֵּילוֹת אָנוּ אוֹכְלִין בֵּין
יוֹשְׁבִין וּבֵין מְסֻבִּין. הַלַּיְלָה הַזֶּה
כֻּלָּנוּ מְסֻבִּין:

We are slaves to Pharaoh
in Egypt, but God brought us
out from there with
a strong hand and
an outstretched arm.
If God had not brought out
our fathers from Egypt,
then we, our children
and our children's children
would have remained enslaved
to Pharaoh in Egypt. Therefore,
even if all of us are wise,
all of us are clever, all Elders
[of our people], all fully versed
in the Torah, we would still
be obligated to recall
the Exodus. Whoever tells about
it at length is praiseworthy.

עֲבָדִים הָיִינוּ לְפַרְעֹה בְּמִצְרַיִם.
וַיּוֹצִיאֵנוּ יְיָ אֱלֹהֵינוּ מִשָּׁם בְּיָד
חֲזָקָה וּבִזְרוֹעַ נְטוּיָה. וְאִלּוּ לֹא
הוֹצִיא הַקָּדוֹשׁ בָּרוּךְ הוּא אֶת־
אֲבוֹתֵינוּ מִמִּצְרַיִם הֲרֵי אָנוּ
וּבָנֵינוּ וּבְנֵי בָנֵינוּ מְשֻׁעְבָּדִים
הָיִינוּ (לְפַרְעֹה) בְּמִצְרַיִם.
וַאֲפִילוּ כֻּלָּנוּ חֲכָמִים. כֻּלָּנוּ
נְבוֹנִים. כֻּלָּנוּ זְקֵנִים. כֻּלָּנוּ
יוֹדְעִים אֶת־הַתּוֹרָה. מִצְוָה
עָלֵינוּ לְסַפֵּר בִּיצִיאַת מִצְרָיִם.
וְכָל־הַמַּרְבֶּה לְסַפֵּר בִּיצִיאַת
מִצְרַיִם הֲרֵי זֶה מְשֻׁבָּח:

Rabbi Eliezer, Rabbi Yehoshua,
Rabbi Elazar son of Azaryah,
Rabbi Akiva and Rabbi Tarfon
were celebrating the Seder
in Bnei Brak. They were
discussing the Exodus the
entire night, until their students
came and said to them:
Rabbis, the time has arrived for
reading the morning Sh'ma.

מַעֲשֶׂה בְּרַבִּי אֱלִיעֶזֶר וְרַבִּי
יְהוֹשֻׁעַ וְרַבִּי אֶלְעָזָר בֶּן עֲזַרְיָה
וְרַבִּי עֲקִיבָא וְרַבִּי טַרְפוֹן שֶׁהָיוּ
מְסֻבִּין בִּבְנֵי בְרַק. וְהָיוּ
מְסַפְּרִים בִּיצִיאַת מִצְרַיִם כָּל־
אוֹתוֹ הַלַּיְלָה. עַד שֶׁבָּאוּ
תַלְמִידֵיהֶם וְאָמְרוּ לָהֶם
רַבּוֹתֵינוּ הִגִּיעַ זְמַן קְרִיאַת
שְׁמַע שֶׁל שַׁחֲרִית:

Rabbi Elazar son of Azaryah
said: I am like a man
of seventy years,
yet I was never able to prove
that one is obliged to mention
the Exodus at night,
until Ben Zoma explained it.
It is written in the Torah:
"That you may remember
the day when you came out
of the land of Egypt,
all the days of your life"

(Deuteronomy 16:3).

"The days of your life"
refers to the days,
"ALL the days of your life"
includes the nights.
The Sages taught:
"The days of your life"
refers to this world,
"ALL the days of your life"
refers to the time of messiah.

אָמַר רַבִּי אֶלְעָזָר בֶּן עֲזַרְיָה.
הֲרֵי אֲנִי כְּבֶן שִׁבְעִים שָׁנָה וְלֹא
זָכִיתִי שֶׁתֵּאָמֵר יְצִיאַת מִצְרַיִם
בַּלֵּילוֹת. עַד שֶׁדְּרָשָׁהּ בֶּן זוֹמָא.
שֶׁנֶּאֱמַר: לְמַעַן תִּזְכֹּר אֶת־יוֹם
צֵאתְךָ מֵאֶרֶץ מִצְרַיִם כֹּל יְמֵי
חַיֶּיךָ. יְמֵי חַיֶּיךָ, הַיָּמִים. כֹּל יְמֵי
חַיֶּיךָ, הַלֵּילוֹת: וַחֲכָמִים אוֹמְרִים
יְמֵי חַיֶּיךָ, הָעוֹלָם הַזֶּה. כֹּל יְמֵי
חַיֶּיךָ, לְהָבִיא לִימוֹת הַמָּשִׁיחַ:

Blessed Ever-Present,
blessed is He.
Blessed is the One
Who has given the Torah
to His people Israel,
blessed is He.

בָּרוּךְ הַמָּקוֹם בָּרוּךְ הוּא.
בָּרוּךְ שֶׁנָּתַן תּוֹרָה לְעַמּוֹ
יִשְׂרָאֵל. בָּרוּךְ הוּא:

The Torah speaks of four sons:
a wise one, a wicked one,
a simple one, and one who
does not know how to ask.

כְּנֶגֶד אַרְבָּעָה בָנִים דִּבְּרָה
תוֹרָה. אֶחָד חָכָם. וְאֶחָד רָשָׁע.
וְאֶחָד תָּם. וְאֶחָד שֶׁאֵינוֹ יוֹדֵעַ
לִשְׁאוֹל:

חָכָם מַה הוּא אוֹמֵר. מָה הָעֵדֹת וְהַחֻקִּים וְהַמִּשְׁפָּטִים אֲשֶׁר צִוָּה יְיָ אֱלֹהֵינוּ אֶתְכֶם: וְאַף אַתָּה אֱמָר־לוֹ כְּהִלְכוֹת הַפֶּסַח. אֵין מַפְטִירִין אַחַר הַפֶּסַח אֲפִיקוֹמָן:

רָשָׁע מַה הוּא אוֹמֵר. מָה הָעֲבֹדָה הַזֹּאת לָכֶם: לָכֶם וְלֹא לוֹ. וּלְפִי שֶׁהוֹצִיא אֶת־עַצְמוֹ מִן הַכְּלָל כָּפַר בָּעִקָּר. וְאַף אַתָּה הַקְהֵה אֶת־שִׁנָּיו וֶאֱמָר־לוֹ: בַּעֲבוּר זֶה עָשָׂה יְיָ לִי בְּצֵאתִי מִמִּצְרָיִם. לִי וְלֹא לוֹ. אִלּוּ הָיָה שָׁם לֹא הָיָה נִגְאָל:

The wise son, what does he say?
"What are the statements, regulations and laws that God has commanded you?" (Deuteronomy 6:20). Instruct him in the laws of Pesach, that after eating the Pesach sacrifice, we do not eat anything!

The wicked son, what does he say?
"What does the service mean to you" (Exodus 12:26). "To you" [he says] but not about himself. Because he has excluded himself from the community, he has denied [the Exodus and] God. Therefore, you must answer bluntly, "Because of this God did for me when I went out from Egypt" (Exodus 13:8). "For me," not for him. Had he been there, he would not have been redeemed.

THE FOUR SONS

תָּם מַה הוּא אוֹמֵר. מַה זֹּאת. וְאָמַרְתָּ אֵלָיו בְּחֹזֶק יָד הוֹצִיאָנוּ יְיָ מִמִּצְרַיִם מִבֵּית עֲבָדִים:

וְשֶׁאֵינוֹ יוֹדֵעַ לִשְׁאוֹל אַתְּ פְּתַח לוֹ. שֶׁנֶּאֱמַר. וְהִגַּדְתָּ לְבִנְךָ בַּיּוֹם הַהוּא לֵאמֹר בַּעֲבוּר זֶה עָשָׂה יְיָ לִי בְּצֵאתִי מִמִּצְרָיִם:

The simple son, what does he say?
"What does [all] this mean?"
To him you shall say,
"With a strong hand God brought us
out from Egypt, from slavery" (Exodus 13:14).

As for the son who does not know
how to ask, you must begin for him,
as is written: "You shall tell
your son on that day 'Because of this,
God did for me when
I went out from Egypt'" (Exodus 13:8).

יָכוֹל מֵרֹאשׁ חֹדֶשׁ. תַּלְמוּד לוֹמַר בַּיוֹם הַהוּא. אִי בַּיוֹם הַהוּא יָכוֹל מִבְּעוֹד יוֹם. תַּלְמוּד לוֹמַר בַּעֲבוּר זֶה. בַּעֲבוּר זֶה לֹא אָמַרְתִּי אֶלָּא בְּשָׁעָה שֶׁיֵּשׁ מַצָּה וּמָרוֹר מֻנָּחִים לְפָנֶיךָ:

מִתְּחִלָּה עוֹבְדֵי עֲבוֹדָה זָרָה הָיוּ אֲבוֹתֵינוּ. וְעַכְשָׁו קֵרְבָנוּ הַמָּקוֹם לַעֲבוֹדָתוֹ. שֶׁנֶּאֱמַר. וַיֹּאמֶר יְהוֹשֻׁעַ אֶל־כָּל־הָעָם. כֹּה־אָמַר יְיָ אֱלֹהֵי יִשְׂרָאֵל בְּעֵבֶר הַנָּהָר יָשְׁבוּ אֲבוֹתֵיכֶם מֵעוֹלָם. תֶּרַח אֲבִי אַבְרָהָם וַאֲבִי נָחוֹר. וַיַּעַבְדוּ אֱלֹהִים אֲחֵרִים:

One might think that the obligation [to recite the story of the Exodus]
applies from the first day of Nissan. Therefore the Torah says:
"On that day." "That day" might be understood [that the Seder is to begin]
during the day. Therefore, the Torah adds, "Because of this"—
only at a time when matzah and maror are before you.

Initially our ancestors were idol worshipers, but now God has brought us
to serve Him. As is written: "And Yehoshua spoke to the people:
God, Lord of Israel, said, Your fathers dwelt on the other side
of the [Euphrates] River, [including] Terach, the father of Avraham
and the father of Nachor, and they served other gods.

A DEEP SLEEP FELL UPON ABRAHAM (GENESIS 15:12)

And I took your father Avraham from beyond the River and led him throughout the land of Canaan, and I multiplied his seed and gave him Yitzchak. And I gave to Yitzchak [two sons], Yaakov and Esav; to Esav I gave Mount Seir, to possess it, but Yaakov and his sons went down to Egypt" (Joshua 24:3,4).

וָאֶקַּח אֶת־אֲבִיכֶם אֶת־אַבְרָהָם מֵעֵבֶר הַנָּהָר. וָאוֹלֵךְ אוֹתוֹ בְּכָל־אֶרֶץ כְּנָעַן. וָאַרְבֶּה אֶת־זַרְעוֹ וָאֶתֶּן־לוֹ אֶת־יִצְחָק: וָאֶתֵּן לְיִצְחָק אֶת־יַעֲקֹב וְאֶת־עֵשָׂו. וָאֶתֵּן לְעֵשָׂו אֶת־הַר שֵׂעִיר לָרֶשֶׁת אוֹתוֹ. וְיַעֲקֹב וּבָנָיו יָרְדוּ מִצְרָיִם:

Blessed is He who keeps His promise to Israel, blessed is He! For the Holy One, blessed is He, planned the end [of their bondage], in order to fulfill what He had said to our father Avraham at the Convenant of the Halves. As is written: "And He said to Avraham: 'You should know for certain that your descendants shall be strangers in a land that is not their own; and they will enslave them, and shall treat them harshly, for four hundred years. But I will also judge the nation that they shall serve, and afterwards they shall leave with great wealth'" (Genesis 15:13-14).

בָּרוּךְ שׁוֹמֵר הַבְטָחָתוֹ לְיִשְׂרָאֵל. בָּרוּךְ הוּא. שֶׁהַקָּדוֹשׁ בָּרוּךְ הוּא חִשַּׁב אֶת־הַקֵּץ. לַעֲשׂוֹת כְּמָה שֶׁאָמַר לְאַבְרָהָם אָבִינוּ בִּבְרִית בֵּין הַבְּתָרִים. שֶׁנֶּאֱמַר. וַיֹּאמֶר לְאַבְרָם יָדֹעַ תֵּדַע כִּי־גֵר יִהְיֶה זַרְעֲךָ בְּאֶרֶץ לֹא לָהֶם וַעֲבָדוּם וְעִנּוּ אֹתָם אַרְבַּע מֵאוֹת שָׁנָה: וְגַם אֶת־הַגּוֹי אֲשֶׁר יַעֲבֹדוּ דָּן אָנֹכִי וְאַחֲרֵי־כֵן יֵצְאוּ בִּרְכֻשׁ גָּדוֹל:

THE MATZOT ARE COVERED,
AND THE CUPS OF WINE ARE LIFTED.

It is this that has stood
by our fathers and us;
for not only one [enemy]
has risen up against us
to destroy us, but in all
generations they rise up
against us to destroy us.
But the Holy One, Blessed is He,
saves us from their hands.

THE CUPS ARE RETURNED TO THE TABLE
AND THE MATZOT UNCOVERED.

Go and learn what Lavan
the Aramean planned to do
to our father Yaakov!
Pharaoh decreed that only
the male children [should be put
to death], but Lavan wanted
to uproot the whole [Jewish
nation], as is written: "The
Aramean sought to destroy
my forefather. He [Yaakov] went
down to Egypt and lived there,
few in number; and there
he became a nation, great,
mighty and numerous"
(Deuteronomy 26:5).

וְהִיא שֶׁעָמְדָה לַאֲבוֹתֵינוּ וְלָנוּ.
שֶׁלֹּא אֶחָד בִּלְבָד עָמַד עָלֵינוּ
לְכַלּוֹתֵנוּ. אֶלָּא שֶׁבְּכָל־דּוֹר וָדוֹר
עוֹמְדִים עָלֵינוּ לְכַלּוֹתֵנוּ.
וְהַקָּדוֹשׁ בָּרוּךְ הוּא מַצִּילֵנוּ
מִיָּדָם:

צֵא וּלְמַד, מַה בִּקֵּשׁ לָבָן
הָאֲרַמִּי לַעֲשׂוֹת לְיַעֲקֹב אָבִינוּ.
שֶׁפַּרְעֹה לֹא גָזַר אֶלָּא עַל
הַזְּכָרִים, וְלָבָן בִּקֵּשׁ לַעֲקֹר אֶת־
הַכֹּל, שֶׁנֶּאֱמַר: אֲרַמִּי אֹבֵד אָבִי,
וַיֵּרֶד מִצְרַיְמָה, וַיָּגָר שָׁם בִּמְתֵי
מְעָט. וַיְהִי שָׁם לְגוֹי גָּדוֹל, עָצוּם
וָרָב:

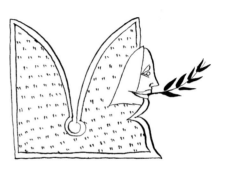

THE PEOPLE CROSS THE RED SEA

"He went down to Egypt"—
impelled, by [God's] word.
"And he lived there"—
this teaches that our father
Yaakov did not go to Egypt
to settle there permanently,
just temporarily, as is written:
"And the sons of Yaakov said
to Pharaoh: 'We have come
to live in this land temporarily,
for there is no pasture
for the flocks that belong
to your servants, for the famine
is harsh in the land of Canaan;
now, please let your servants
dwell in the land of Goshen'"
(Genesis 47:4).
"Few in number"—as is written:
"With seventy souls your fathers
went down to Egypt, and now
God has made you as numerous
as the stars of heaven"
(Deuteronomy 10:22).
"And there he became
a nation"—which teaches that
the Jews were distinctive there.
"Great, mighty"—as is written:
"And the children of Israel
were fruitful and increased
abundantly and multiplied.
And they became very,
very mighty; and the land
was filled with them" (Exodus 1:7).

וַיֵּרֶד מִצְרַיְמָה. אָנוּם עַל פִּי
הַדִּבּוּר: וַיָּגָר שָׁם. מְלַמֵּד שֶׁלֹּא
יָרַד יַעֲקֹב אָבִינוּ לְהִשְׁתַּקֵּעַ
בְּמִצְרַיִם אֶלָּא לָגוּר שָׁם.
שֶׁנֶּאֱמַר. וַיֹּאמְרוּ אֶל־פַּרְעֹה
לָגוּר בָּאָרֶץ בָּאנוּ כִּי־אֵין מִרְעֶה
לַצֹּאן אֲשֶׁר לַעֲבָדֶיךָ כִּי כָבֵד
הָרָעָב בְּאֶרֶץ כְּנָעַן וְעַתָּה יֵשְׁבוּ
נָא עֲבָדֶיךָ בְּאֶרֶץ גֹּשֶׁן: בִּמְתֵי
מְעָט. כְּמָה שֶׁנֶּאֱמַר. בְּשִׁבְעִים
נֶפֶשׁ יָרְדוּ אֲבֹתֶיךָ מִצְרַיְמָה
וְעַתָּה שָׂמְךָ יְיָ אֱלֹהֶיךָ כְּכוֹכְבֵי
הַשָּׁמַיִם לָרֹב: וַיְהִי שָׁם לְגוֹי
גָּדוֹל. מְלַמֵּד שֶׁהָיוּ יִשְׂרָאֵל
מְצֻיָּנִים שָׁם: עָצוּם. כְּמָה
שֶׁנֶּאֱמַר. וּבְנֵי יִשְׂרָאֵל פָּרוּ
וַיִּשְׁרְצוּ וַיִּרְבּוּ וַיַּעַצְמוּ בִּמְאֹד
מְאֹד וַתִּמָּלֵא הָאָרֶץ אֹתָם:

"And numerous"—as is written: "I caused you to increase like the plants of the field; you increased and grew tall, and you matured. Your form was full, your hair was grown, but you were naked and bare. I passed over you and saw you covered with your blood, and I said to you: 'Through your blood you shall live'; and I said to you: 'Through your blood you shall live'" (Ezekiel 16:6-7).

"The Egyptians did evil to us. They oppressed us and laid heavy labors upon us" (Deuteronomy 26:6).

"The Egyptians did evil to us"—as is written: "Let us deal cunningly with them, lest they multiply. If we should happen to be beset by war, they will join our enemies, fight against us, and leave the land" (Exodus 1:10).

"They oppressed us"—as is written: "They placed taskmasters over them, to oppress them with their burdens, and they built storage cities for Pharaoh, [the cities] of Pisom and Ramses" (Exodus 1:11).

"They laid heavy labors upon us"—as is written: "The Egyptians forced the children of Israel to do slave labor" (Exodus 1:13).

וָרָב. כְּמָה שֶׁנֶּאֱמַר. רְבָבָה כְּצֶמַח הַשָּׂדֶה נְתַתִּיךְ וַתִּרְבִּי וַתִּגְדְּלִי וַתָּבֹאִי בַּעֲדִי עֲדָיִים שָׁדַיִם נָכֹנוּ וּשְׂעָרֵךְ צִמֵּחַ וְאַתְּ עֵרֹם וְעֶרְיָה:

וַיָּרֵעוּ אֹתָנוּ הַמִּצְרִים וַיְעַנּוּנוּ. וַיִּתְּנוּ עָלֵינוּ עֲבֹדָה קָשָׁה: וַיָּרֵעוּ אֹתָנוּ הַמִּצְרִים. כְּמָה שֶׁנֶּאֱמַר. הָבָה נִתְחַכְּמָה לֹו. פֶּן־יִרְבֶּה וְהָיָה כִּי־תִקְרֶאנָה מִלְחָמָה וְנֹוסַף גַּם־הוּא עַל־ שֹׂנְאֵינוּ וְנִלְחַם־בָּנוּ וְעָלָה מִן־ הָאָרֶץ: וַיְעַנּוּנוּ. כְּמָה שֶׁנֶּאֱמַר. וַיָּשִׂימוּ עָלָיו שָׂרֵי מִסִּים לְמַעַן עַנֹּתֹו בְּסִבְלֹתָם וַיִּבֶן עָרֵי מִסְכְּנֹות לְפַרְעֹה אֶת־פִּתֹם וְאֶת־רַעַמְסֵס: וַיִּתְּנוּ עָלֵינוּ עֲבֹדָה קָשָׁה. כְּמָה שֶׁנֶּאֱמַר. וַיַּעֲבִדוּ מִצְרַיִם אֶת־ בְּנֵי יִשְׂרָאֵל בְּפָרֶךְ:

"And we cried out to God, the God of our fathers. And He heard our voice, and He saw our suffering, our burden and our oppression" (Deuteronomy 26:7).

"And we cried out to God, the God of our fathers"— as is written: "And it came to pass during that long period, that the king of Egypt died. The children of Israel moaned because of the hard labor, and they cried out. And from the bondage their prayers rose up to God" (Exodus 2:23). "And God heard our voice"— as is written: "God heard their groaning and God recalled His convenant with Avraham, Yitzchak, and Yaakov" (Exodus 2:24). "And He saw our suffering"— this refers to the separation of husband and wife, as is written: "God saw the children of Israel and God knew" (Exodus 2:25). "Our burden"—these are the children, as is written: "Every newborn son you shall throw into the Nile river, but every daughter you shall let live" (Exodus 1:22).

וַנִּצְעַק אֶל־יְיָ אֱלֹהֵי אֲבֹתֵינוּ וַיִּשְׁמַע יְיָ אֶת־קֹלֵנוּ וַיַּרְא אֶת־עָנְיֵנוּ וְאֶת־עֲמָלֵנוּ וְאֶת לַחֲצֵנוּ: וַנִּצְעַק אֶל־יְיָ אֱלֹהֵי אֲבֹתֵינוּ. כְּמָה שֶׁנֶּאֱמַר. וַיְהִי בַיָּמִים הָרַבִּים הָהֵם וַיָּמָת מֶלֶךְ מִצְרַיִם וַיֵּאָנְחוּ בְנֵי־יִשְׂרָאֵל מִן הָעֲבֹדָה וַיִּזְעָקוּ וַתַּעַל שַׁוְעָתָם אֶל־הָאֱלֹהִים מִן־הָעֲבֹדָה: וַיִּשְׁמַע יְיָ אֶת קֹלֵנוּ. כְּמָה שֶׁנֶּאֱמַר. וַיִּשְׁמַע אֱלֹהִים אֶת־נַאֲקָתָם וַיִּזְכֹּר אֱלֹהִים אֶת־בְּרִיתוֹ אֶת־אַבְרָהָם אֶת־יִצְחָק וְאֶת־יַעֲקֹב: וַיַּרְא אֶת עָנְיֵנוּ. זוֹ פְּרִישׁוּת דֶּרֶךְ אֶרֶץ. כְּמָה שֶׁנֶּאֱמַר. וַיַּרְא אֱלֹהִים אֶת־בְּנֵי יִשְׂרָאֵל. וַיֵּדַע אֱלֹהִים: וְאֶת עֲמָלֵנוּ. אֵלוּ הַבָּנִים. כְּמָה שֶׁנֶּאֱמַר. כָּל־הַבֵּן הַיִּלּוֹד הַיְאֹרָה תַּשְׁלִיכֻהוּ וְכָל־הַבַּת תְּחַיּוּן:

"And our oppression"–
this was the pressure [placed
upon the Jews] as is written:
"I have also seen the oppression
with which the Egyptians
oppress them" (Exodus 3:9).
"God brought us out of Egypt
with a mighty hand,
with an outstretched arm,
with great fear, with signs and
with wonders" (Deuteronomy 26:8).
"God brought us out of Egypt"–
not through an angel,
not through a seraph
and not through a messenger.
It was the Holy One,
Blessed is He, alone and
in His glory. As is written:
"On that night I will pass
through the land of Egypt
and I will slay every firstborn
in the land of Egypt, from man
to beast, and all the gods
of Egypt I will judge,
[for] I am God" (Exodus 12:12).
"On that night I will pass
through the land of Egypt"–
I, and not an angel; "And I will
slay every first-born in the land
of Egypt"–I, and not a seraph;
"And all the gods of Egypt I will
judge"–I, and not a messenger;
"[for] I am God"–I, and no other.

וְאֶת לַחֲצֵנוּ. זֶה הַדְּחַק. כְּמָה
שֶׁנֶּאֱמַר. וְגַם־רָאִיתִי אֶת־הַלַּחַץ
אֲשֶׁר מִצְרַיִם לֹחֲצִים אֹתָם:

וַיּוֹצִאֵנוּ יְיָ מִמִּצְרַיִם, בְּיָד חֲזָקָה
וּבִזְרֹעַ נְטוּיָה וּבְמֹרָא גָּדוֹל
וּבְאֹתוֹת וּבְמוֹפְתִים:
וַיּוֹצִאֵנוּ יְיָ מִמִּצְרַיִם. לֹא עַל יְדֵי
מַלְאָךְ. וְלֹא עַל יְדֵי שָׂרָף. וְלֹא
עַל יְדֵי שָׁלִיחַ. אֶלָּא הַקָּדוֹשׁ
בָּרוּךְ הוּא בִּכְבוֹדוֹ וּבְעַצְמוֹ.
שֶׁנֶּאֱמַר. וְעָבַרְתִּי בְאֶרֶץ
מִצְרַיִם בַּלַּיְלָה הַזֶּה וְהִכֵּיתִי
כָל־בְּכוֹר בְּאֶרֶץ מִצְרַיִם מֵאָדָם
וְעַד־בְּהֵמָה וּבְכָל־אֱלֹהֵי מִצְרַיִם
אֶעֱשֶׂה שְׁפָטִים אֲנִי יְיָ: וְעָבַרְתִּי
בְאֶרֶץ־מִצְרַיִם. אֲנִי וְלֹא מַלְאָךְ.
וְהִכֵּיתִי כָל בְּכוֹר. אֲנִי וְלֹא
שָׂרָף. וּבְכָל־אֱלֹהֵי מִצְרַיִם
אֶעֱשֶׂה שְׁפָטִים. אֲנִי וְלֹא
הַשָּׁלִיחַ. אֲנִי יְיָ. אֲנִי הוּא וְלֹא
אַחֵר:

בְּיָד חֲזָקָה. זוֹ הַדֶּבֶר. כְּמָה שֶׁנֶּאֱמַר. הִנֵּה יַד־יְיָ הוֹיָה בְּמִקְנְךָ אֲשֶׁר בַּשָּׂדֶה בַּסּוּסִים בַּחֲמֹרִים בַּגְּמַלִּים, בַּבָּקָר וּבַצֹּאן דֶּבֶר כָּבֵד מְאֹד:

וּבִזְרֹעַ נְטוּיָה. זוֹ הַחֶרֶב. כְּמָה שֶׁנֶּאֱמַר: וְחַרְבּוֹ שְׁלוּפָה בְּיָדוֹ, נְטוּיָה עַל־יְרוּשָׁלַיִם:

וּבְמוֹרָא גָּדוֹל. זוֹ גִּלּוּי שְׁכִינָה. כְּמָה שֶׁנֶּאֱמַר. אוֹ הֲנִסָּה אֱלֹהִים לָבוֹא לָקַחַת לוֹ גוֹי מִקֶּרֶב גּוֹי בְּמַסֹּת בְּאֹתֹת וּבְמוֹפְתִים וּבְמִלְחָמָה וּבְיָד חֲזָקָה וּבִזְרוֹעַ נְטוּיָה וּבְמוֹרָאִים גְּדֹלִים כְּכֹל אֲשֶׁר־עָשָׂה לָכֶם יְיָ אֱלֹהֵיכֶם בְּמִצְרַיִם לְעֵינֶיךָ:

"With a mighty hand"—this
is [the plague of] pestilence,
as is written: "Behold! God's
Hand will be upon your
livestock in the field, upon
the horses, mules and camels,
the cattle and the sheep, a very
severe pestilence" (Exodus 9:3).
"With an outstretched arm"—
this is the sword, as is written:
"His sword was drawn in his
hand, stretched out over
Jerusalem" (1 Chronicles 21:16).
"With great fear"—this is the
revelation of the Divine Presence,
as is written: "Or has God ever
attempted to take unto Himself
one nation from amidst another
nation, with trials, signs and
wonders; with war, a mighty
hand, and an outstretched arm
and with great fear, as God
did for you in Egypt before
your eyes?" (Deuteronomy 4:34).

וּבְאֹתוֹת. זֶה הַמַּטֶּה. כְּמָה שֶׁנֶּאֱמַר. וְאֶת הַמַּטֶּה הַזֶּה
תִּקַּח בְּיָדֶךָ אֲשֶׁר תַּעֲשֶׂה־בּוֹ אֶת־הָאֹתֹת:
וּבְמֹפְתִים. זֶה הַדָּם. כְּמָה שֶׁנֶּאֱמַר. וְנָתַתִּי מוֹפְתִים
בַּשָּׁמַיִם וּבָאָרֶץ: דָּם. וָאֵשׁ. וְתִימְרוֹת עָשָׁן:

דָּבָר אַחֵר. בְּיָד חֲזָקָה שְׁתַּיִם. וּבִזְרֹעַ נְטוּיָה שְׁתַּיִם.
וּבְמוֹרָא גָדוֹל שְׁתַּיִם. וּבְאֹתוֹת שְׁתַּיִם. וּבְמֹפְתִים שְׁתַּיִם:

"With signs"—this refers
to the staff, as is written:
"Take this staff in your hand,
with which you shall
perform the signs" (Exodus 4:17).
"And with wonders"—
this is blood, as is written:
"I will show wonders in heaven
and on earth. Blood, and fire,
and pillars of smoke" (Joel 3:3).

Another explanation [of the
verse]: "With a mighty hand"—
indicates two plagues;
"With an outstretched arm"—
another two;
"With great fear"—
another two; "With signs"—
another two;
"And wonders"—
another two.

אֵלּוּ עֶשֶׂר מַכּוֹת שֶׁהֵבִיא הַקָּדוֹשׁ
בָּרוּךְ הוּא עַל־הַמִּצְרִים בְּמִצְרַיִם:
וְאֵלּוּ הֵן.

דָּם. צְפַרְדֵּעַ. כִּנִּים.
עָרוֹב. דֶּבֶר. שְׁחִין.
בָּרָד. אַרְבֶּה. חֹשֶׁךְ.
מַכַּת בְּכוֹרוֹת:

רַבִּי יְהוּדָה הָיָה נוֹתֵן בָּהֶם סִמָּנִים.
דְּצַ"ךְ עֲדַ"שׁ בְּאַחַ"ב:

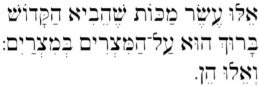

These are the Ten Plagues
which the Holy One, Blessed is He,
brought upon the Egyptians
in Egypt, namely:

WHEN RECITING EACH OF THESE PUNISHMENTS
AND AGAIN WHEN RECITING THE PLAGUES,
POUR SOME WINE FROM THE CUP (WITH A FINGER OR A SPOON).

Blood; Frogs; Lice;
Wild Animals; Pestilence; Boils;
Hail; Locusts; Darkness;
Slaying of the Firstborn.

Rabbi Yehudah grouped them by their
Hebrew initials: DeTZaKH, ADaSH, B'ACHaB.

רַבִּי יוֹסֵי הַגְּלִילִי
אוֹמֵר. מִנַּיִן אַתָּה
אוֹמֵר שֶׁלָּקוּ
הַמִּצְרִיִּים בְּמִצְרַיִם
עֶשֶׂר מַכּוֹת. וְעַל
הַיָּם לָקוּ חֲמִשִּׁים
מַכּוֹת. בְּמִצְרַיִם
מָה הוּא אוֹמֵר.
וַיֹּאמְרוּ הַחַרְטֻמִּם
אֶל־פַּרְעֹה אֶצְבַּע
אֱלֹהִים הוּא: וְעַל הַיָּם מָה הוּא
אוֹמֵר. וַיַּרְא יִשְׂרָאֵל אֶת־הַיָּד
הַגְּדֹלָה אֲשֶׁר עָשָׂה יְיָ בְּמִצְרַיִם
וַיִּירְאוּ הָעָם אֶת־יְיָ וַיַּאֲמִינוּ בַּיְיָ
וּבְמֹשֶׁה עַבְדּוֹ:

REFILL THE CUP.

Rabbi Yosi the Galilean said:
From where do we know
that the Egyptians were struck
by ten plagues in Egypt,
but by fifty plagues at the Sea?
About Egypt it is written: And
the magicians said to Pharaoh, It
is the finger of God (Exodus 8:15).
About the Red Sea it is written:
"When Israel saw the great hand
which God directed against
the Egyptians, the people feared
God, and believed in God and in
His servant Moshe" (Exodus 14:31).

How many plagues did they
receive with the finger (of God)?
Ten! It follows that since
there were ten plagues in Egypt,
there were fifty at the Red Sea
(where they were
struck with a hand).

Rabbi Eiezer said; From where
do we know that each plague
that the Holy One,
Blessed is He, visited
upon the Egyptians in Egypt
consisted of four plagues?
It is written: "He sent forth
upon them His burning anger:
fury, rage, trouble, and
messengers of evil" (Psalms 78:49).
Fury is one, Rage, two.
Trouble, three and
Messengers of evil, four.
Thus, they were struck
by forty plagues in Egypt,
and two hundred at the Sea.

Rabbi Akiva said: From where
do we know that each plague
that the Holy One, Blessed is He,
visited upon the Egyptians in
Egypt consisted of five plagues?

כַּמָּה לָקוּ בְּאֶצְבַּע. עֶשֶׂר מַכּוֹת.
אֱמֹר מֵעַתָּה בְּמִצְרַיִם לָקוּ
עֶשֶׂר מַכּוֹת וְעַל־הַיָּם לָקוּ
חֲמִשִּׁים מַכּוֹת:

רַבִּי אֱלִיעֶזֶר אוֹמֵר. מִנַּיִן
שֶׁכָּל־מַכָּה וּמַכָּה שֶׁהֵבִיא
הַקָּדוֹשׁ בָּרוּךְ הוּא עַל הַמִּצְרִים
בְּמִצְרַיִם הָיְתָה שֶׁל אַרְבַּע
מַכּוֹת. שֶׁנֶּאֱמַר. יְשַׁלַּח־בָּם חֲרוֹן
אַפּוֹ עֶבְרָה וָזַעַם וְצָרָה
מִשְׁלַחַת מַלְאֲכֵי רָעִים: עֶבְרָה
אַחַת. וָזַעַם שְׁתַּיִם. וְצָרָה
שָׁלֹשׁ. מִשְׁלַחַת מַלְאֲכֵי רָעִים
אַרְבַּע. אֱמוֹר מֵעַתָּה בְּמִצְרַיִם
לָקוּ אַרְבָּעִים מַכּוֹת וְעַל הַיָּם
לָקוּ מָאתַיִם מַכּוֹת:

רַבִּי עֲקִיבָא אוֹמֵר. מִנַּיִן שֶׁכָּל־
מַכָּה וּמַכָּה שֶׁהֵבִיא הַקָּדוֹשׁ
בָּרוּךְ הוּא עַל הַמִּצְרִיִּים
בְּמִצְרַיִם הָיְתָה שֶׁל חָמֵשׁ
מַכּוֹת.

It is written: "He sent forth upon them His burning anger, fury, rage, trouble, and messengers of evil (Ibid.). Burning anger is one. Fury, two. Rage, three. Trouble, four. And Messengers of evil, five. Thus, they were struck by fifty plagues in Egypt, and two hundred and fifty at the Sea.

שֶׁנֶּאֱמַר יְשַׁלַּח־בָּם חֲרוֹן אַפּוֹ עֶבְרָה וָזַעַם וְצָרָה מִשְׁלַחַת מַלְאֲכֵי רָעִים. חֲרוֹן אַפּוֹ אַחַת. עֶבְרָה שְׁתַּיִם. וָזַעַם שָׁלֹשׁ. וְצָרָה אַרְבַּע. מִשְׁלַחַת מַלְאֲכֵי רָעִים חָמֵשׁ. אֱמוֹר מֵעַתָּה בְּמִצְרַיִם לָקוּ חֲמִשִּׁים מַכּוֹת. וְעַל־הַיָּם לָקוּ חֲמִשִּׁים וּמָאתַיִם מַכּוֹת:

The Ever-present has bestowed so many favors upon us! If He had brought us out of Egypt, but had not judged the Egyptians—
Dayeinu,
it would have been enough!
If He had judged them, but not their idols—
Dayeinu!
If He had judged their idols, but not slain their firstborn—
Dayeinu!
If He had slain their firstborn, but not given us their wealth—
Dayeinu!
If He had given us their wealth, but not split the Red Sea before us—
Dayeinu!

כַּמָּה מַעֲלוֹת טוֹבוֹת לַמָּקוֹם עָלֵינוּ:
אִלּוּ הוֹצִיאָנוּ מִמִּצְרַיִם.
וְלֹא עָשָׂה בָהֶם שְׁפָטִים. דַּיֵּנוּ:
אִלּוּ עָשָׂה בָהֶם שְׁפָטִים.
וְלֹא עָשָׂה בֵאלֹהֵיהֶם. דַּיֵּנוּ:
אִלּוּ עָשָׂה בֵאלֹהֵיהֶם.
וְלֹא הָרַג אֶת־בְּכוֹרֵיהֶם. דַּיֵּנוּ:
אִלּוּ הָרַג אֶת־בְּכוֹרֵיהֶם.
וְלֹא נָתַן לָנוּ אֶת־מָמוֹנָם. דַּיֵּנוּ:
אִלּוּ נָתַן לָנוּ אֶת־מָמוֹנָם.
וְלֹא קָרַע לָנוּ אֶת־הַיָּם. דַּיֵּנוּ:

If He had split the Sea,
but not taken us
through it on dry land—
Dayeinu!
If He had led us through the sea
on dry land, but not drowned
our oppressors in it—
Dayeinu!
If He had drowned
our oppressors in it, but had
not provided for our needs in
the wilderness for forty years—
Dayeinu!
If He had provided for our
needs in the wilderness for forty
years, but not fed us manna—
Dayeinu!
If He had fed us manna,
but not given us the Shabbat—
Dayeinu!
If He had given us the Shabbat,
but not led us to Mount Sinai—
Dayeinu!
If He had led us to Mount Sinai,
but not given us the Torah—
Dayeinu!
If He had given us the Torah,
but not brought us
into the Land of Israel—
Dayeinu!
If He had brought us into
the Land of Israel, but not
built a Holy Temple for us—
Dayeinu!

אִלּוּ קָרַע לָנוּ אֶת־הַיָּם. וְלֹא
הֶעֱבִירָנוּ בְתוֹכוֹ בֶּחָרָבָה. דַּיֵּנוּ:
אִלּוּ הֶעֱבִירָנוּ בְתוֹכוֹ בֶּחָרָבָה.
וְלֹא שִׁקַּע צָרֵינוּ בְּתוֹכוֹ. דַּיֵּנוּ:
אִלּוּ שִׁקַּע צָרֵינוּ בְּתוֹכוֹ.
וְלֹא סִפֵּק צָרְכֵּנוּ בַּמִּדְבָּר
אַרְבָּעִים שָׁנָה. דַּיֵּנוּ:
אִלּוּ סִפֵּק צָרְכֵּנוּ בַּמִּדְבָּר
אַרְבָּעִים שָׁנָה.
וְלֹא הֶאֱכִילָנוּ אֶת־הַמָּן. דַּיֵּנוּ:
אִלּוּ הֶאֱכִילָנוּ אֶת־הַמָּן.
וְלֹא נָתַן לָנוּ אֶת־הַשַּׁבָּת. דַּיֵּנוּ:
אִלּוּ נָתַן לָנוּ אֶת־הַשַּׁבָּת.
וְלֹא קֵרְבָנוּ לִפְנֵי הַר סִינַי. דַּיֵּנוּ:
אִלּוּ קֵרְבָנוּ לִפְנֵי הַר סִינַי.
וְלֹא נָתַן לָנוּ אֶת־הַתּוֹרָה. דַּיֵּנוּ:
אִלּוּ נָתַן לָנוּ אֶת־הַתּוֹרָה.
וְלֹא הִכְנִיסָנוּ לְאֶרֶץ
יִשְׂרָאֵל. דַּיֵּנוּ:
אִלּוּ הִכְנִיסָנוּ לְאֶרֶץ יִשְׂרָאֵל.
וְלֹא בָנָה לָנוּ אֶת־בֵּית
הַבְּחִירָה. דַּיֵּנוּ:

Therefore, how much more
so do we owe thanks to the
Ever-Present for all His many,
many favors! He brought us
out of Egypt, judged the
Egyptians, judged their idols,
slew their firstborn, gave us
their wealth, split the Sea for us,
led us through it on dry land,
drowned our oppressors in it,
supplied our needs in the
wilderness for forty years,
fed us manna, gave us
the Shabbat, brought us to
Mount Sinai, gave us the Torah,
brought us to the Land of Israel,
and built us a Holy Temple
to atone for all our sins.

עַל אַחַת כַּמָּה וְכַמָּה טוֹבָה
כְפוּלָה וּמְכֻפֶּלֶת לַמָּקוֹם עָלֵינוּ.
שֶׁהוֹצִיאָנוּ מִמִּצְרַיִם. וְעָשָׂה
בָהֶם שְׁפָטִים. וְעָשָׂה
בֵאלֹהֵיהֶם. וְהָרַג בְּכוֹרֵיהֶם.
וְנָתַן לָנוּ אֶת־מָמוֹנָם. וְקָרַע לָנוּ
אֶת־הַיָּם. וְהֶעֱבִירָנוּ בְתוֹכוֹ
בֶּחָרָבָה. וְשִׁקַּע צָרֵינוּ בְּתוֹכוֹ.
וְסִפֵּק צָרְכֵּנוּ בַּמִּדְבָּר אַרְבָּעִים
שָׁנָה. וְהֶאֱכִילָנוּ אֶת־הַמָּן. וְנָתַן
לָנוּ אֶת־הַשַּׁבָּת. וְקֵרְבָנוּ לִפְנֵי
הַר סִינַי. וְנָתַן לָנוּ אֶת־הַתּוֹרָה.
וְהִכְנִיסָנוּ לְאֶרֶץ יִשְׂרָאֵל. וּבָנָה
לָנוּ אֶת־בֵּית הַבְּחִירָה. לְכַפֵּר
עַל כָּל־עֲוֹנוֹתֵינוּ:

Rabbi Gamliel used to say:
"Whoever does not make clear
(the reasons for) the following
three things at the Pesach Seder
has not fulfilled his obligation
(of maggid): The paschal lamb,
the matzah, and the maror."

NOW LOOK AT THE BONE ON THE SEDER PLATE
(BUT DON'T POINT AT IT OR LIFT IT),
AND THEN SAY THE FOLLOWING:

The paschal lamb that our
fathers ate when the Holy
Temple was still standing—
what was the reason for it?
It was because the Holy One,
Blessed is He, passed over the
houses of our fathers in Egypt,
as it written: "You shall say, it is a
Pesach sacrifice to God, because
He passed over the houses of
the Children of Israel in Egypt.
He struck the Egyptians,
but He saved our households;
and the people kneeled
and bowed down" (Exodus 12:27).

THE MATZAH IS HELD UP FOR ALL TO SEE
AND THE FOLLOWING IS RECITED:

This matzah that we eat—
what is the reason for it?
It is because the dough
of our fathers did not have time
to become chametz
before God revealed Himself
to them and redeemed them,

רַבָּן גַּמְלִיאֵל הָיָה אוֹמֵר. כָּל־
שֶׁלֹּא אָמַר שְׁלֹשָׁה דְבָרִים אֵלּוּ
בַּפֶּסַח לֹא יָצָא יְדֵי חוֹבָתוֹ.
וְאֵלּוּ הֵן: פֶּסַח. מַצָּה וּמָרוֹר:

פֶּסַח שֶׁהָיוּ אֲבוֹתֵינוּ אוֹכְלִים
בִּזְמַן שֶׁבֵּית הַמִּקְדָּשׁ הָיָה קַיָּם
עַל שׁוּם מָה. עַל שׁוּם שֶׁפָּסַח
הַקָּדוֹשׁ בָּרוּךְ הוּא עַל בָּתֵּי
אֲבוֹתֵינוּ בְּמִצְרַיִם. שֶׁנֶּאֱמַר.
וַאֲמַרְתֶּם זֶבַח־פֶּסַח הוּא לַיְיָ
אֲשֶׁר פָּסַח עַל־בָּתֵּי בְנֵי־יִשְׂרָאֵל
בְּמִצְרַיִם בְּנָגְפּוֹ אֶת־מִצְרַיִם
וְאֶת־בָּתֵּינוּ הִצִּיל וַיִּקֹּד הָעָם
וַיִּשְׁתַּחֲווּ:

מַצָּה זוֹ שֶׁאָנוּ אוֹכְלִים עַל שׁוּם
מָה. עַל שׁוּם שֶׁלֹּא הִסְפִּיק
בְּצֵקָם שֶׁל אֲבוֹתֵינוּ לְהַחֲמִיץ
עַד שֶׁנִּגְלָה עֲלֵיהֶם מֶלֶךְ מַלְכֵי
הַמְּלָכִים הַקָּדוֹשׁ בָּרוּךְ הוּא
וּגְאָלָם.

as is written: "And they baked matzah from the dough which they had taken with them from Egypt; it did not become chametz, because they were driven out of Egypt and could not wait. Neither had they prepared any provisions for themselves for the way" (Exodus 12:39).

שֶׁנֶּאֱמַר . וַיֹּאפוּ אֶת־הַבָּצֵק אֲשֶׁר הוֹצִיאוּ מִמִּצְרַיִם, עֻגֹת מַצּוֹת כִּי לֹא חָמֵץ כִּי־גֹרְשׁוּ מִמִּצְרַיִם וְלֹא יָכְלוּ לְהִתְמַהְמֵהַּ וְגַם־צֵדָה לֹא־עָשׂוּ לָהֶם:

THE MAROR IS HELD UP FOR ALL TO SEE AND THE FOLLOWING IS RECITED:

This maror that we eat— what is the reason for it? It is because the Egyptians made the lives of our fathers bitter in Egypt, as is written: "They embittered their lives with hard work; (working with) mortar and bricks, and through all kinds of field work; all their hard labor at which they made them slaves" (Exodus 1:14).

מָרוֹר זֶה שֶׁאָנוּ אוֹכְלִים עַל שׁוּם מָה. עַל שׁוּם שֶׁמֵּרְרוּ הַמִּצְרִים אֶת־חַיֵּי אֲבוֹתֵינוּ בְּמִצְרָיִם. שֶׁנֶּאֱמַר. וַיְמָרְרוּ אֶת־חַיֵּיהֶם בַּעֲבֹדָה קָשָׁה בְּחֹמֶר וּבִלְבֵנִים וּבְכָל־עֲבֹדָה בַּשָּׂדֶה אֵת כָּל־עֲבֹדָתָם אֲשֶׁר עָבְדוּ בָהֶם בְּפָרֶךְ:

In every generation one must regard himself as though he personally had gone out from Egypt, as it is written: "You shall tell your son on that day, Because of this, God did for me when I went out from Egypt" (Exodus 13:8).

בְּכָל דּוֹר וָדוֹר חַיָּב אָדָם לִרְאוֹת אֶת־עַצְמוֹ כְּאִלּוּ הוּא יָצָא מִמִּצְרַיִם. שֶׁנֶּאֱמַר. וְהִגַּדְתָּ לְבִנְךָ בַּיּוֹם הַהוּא לֵאמֹר בַּעֲבוּר זֶה עָשָׂה יְיָ לִי בְּצֵאתִי מִמִּצְרָיִם:

It was not only our fathers
that God redeemed, but
He also redeemed us
with them, as is written:
"And He brought us out
from there, so that He might
lead us and give us
the Land which He had
promised to our fathers"

THE MATZOT ARE COVERED
AND THE CUP IS HELD

Therefore it is our duty to thank,
to praise, to esteem, to glorify,
to exalt, to honor, to beautify,
to extol and pay tribute to the
One Who has performed all
these miracles for our fathers
and for us. He led us from
slavery to freedom; from sorrow
to joy; from mourning
to festivity; from darkness
to bright light; and from
bondage to redemption!
Let us therefore sing before
Him a new song, Hallelu-Yah!

לֹא אֶת־אֲבוֹתֵינוּ בִּלְבָד גָּאַל
הַקָּדוֹשׁ בָּרוּךְ הוּא. אֶלָּא אַף
אוֹתָנוּ גָּאַל עִמָּהֶם. שֶׁנֶּאֱמַר.
וְאוֹתָנוּ הוֹצִיא מִשָּׁם לְמַעַן
הָבִיא אֹתָנוּ, לָתֶת לָנוּ אֶת־
הָאָרֶץ אֲשֶׁר נִשְׁבַּע לַאֲבֹתֵינוּ:

לְפִיכָךְ אֲנַחְנוּ חַיָּבִים לְהוֹדוֹת
לְהַלֵּל לְשַׁבֵּחַ לְפָאֵר לְרוֹמֵם
לְהַדֵּר לְבָרֵךְ לְעַלֵּה וּלְקַלֵּס. לְמִי
שֶׁעָשָׂה לַאֲבוֹתֵינוּ וְלָנוּ אֶת־כָּל־
הַנִּסִּים הָאֵלֶּה. הוֹצִיאָנוּ
מֵעַבְדוּת לְחֵרוּת. מִיָּגוֹן
לְשִׂמְחָה. מֵאֵבֶל לְיוֹם טוֹב.
וּמֵאֲפֵלָה לְאוֹר גָּדוֹל. וּמִשְׁעַבּוּד
לִגְאֻלָּה וְנֹאמַר לְפָנָיו (שִׁירָה
חֲדָשָׁה) הַלְלוּיָהּ:

JACOB'S DREAM (GENESIS 28:12)

הַלְלוּיָהּ הַלְלוּ עַבְדֵי יְיָ. הַלְלוּ אֶת־שֵׁם יְיָ: יְהִי שֵׁם יְיָ
מְבֹרָךְ. מֵעַתָּה וְעַד עוֹלָם: מִמִּזְרַח־שֶׁמֶשׁ עַד־מְבוֹאוֹ. מְהֻלָּל
שֵׁם יְיָ. רָם עַל־כָּל־גּוֹיִם יְיָ. עַל־הַשָּׁמַיִם כְּבוֹדוֹ: מִי כַּיְיָ
אֱלֹהֵינוּ. הַמַּגְבִּיהִי לָשָׁבֶת: הַמַּשְׁפִּילִי לִרְאוֹת. בַּשָּׁמַיִם
וּבָאָרֶץ: מְקִימִי מֵעָפָר דָּל. מֵאַשְׁפֹּת יָרִים אֶבְיוֹן: לְהוֹשִׁיבִי
עִם־נְדִיבִים. עִם נְדִיבֵי עַמּוֹ: מוֹשִׁיבִי עֲקֶרֶת הַבַּיִת אֵם־
הַבָּנִים שְׂמֵחָה. הַלְלוּיָהּ:

THE MANNA (EXODUS 15:15)

THE CUP IS REPLACED AND THE MATZOT UNCOVERED.

Hallelu-Yah! Praise, you servants
of God, praise the Name of God!
Blessed is the Name of God, from
now and forever. From the rising
of the sun until its setting, let God's
Name be praised. High above all
nations is God, His glory is above
the heavens. Who is like God,
our God, Whose throne is on high,
yet He looks down so low to see the
heavens and the earth! He raises up
the poor out of the dust, lifts up the
needy from the dunghill; in order to
seat him with princes, with the princes
of His people. He turns a barren
housewife into a joyful mother
of children, Hallelu-Yah! (Psalms 113).

בְּצֵאת יִשְׂרָאֵל מִמִּצְרָיִם. בֵּית יַעֲקֹב מֵעַם לֹעֵז: הָיְתָה
יְהוּדָה לְקָדְשׁוֹ. יִשְׂרָאֵל מַמְשְׁלוֹתָיו: הַיָּם רָאָה וַיָּנֹס. הַיַּרְדֵּן
יִסֹּב לְאָחוֹר: הֶהָרִים רָקְדוּ כְאֵילִים. גְּבָעוֹת כִּבְנֵי־צֹאן: מַה־
לְּךָ הַיָּם כִּי תָנוּס. הַיַּרְדֵּן תִּסֹּב לְאָחוֹר: הֶהָרִים תִּרְקְדוּ
כְאֵילִים. גְּבָעוֹת כִּבְנֵי־צֹאן: מִלִּפְנֵי אָדוֹן חוּלִי אָרֶץ. מִלִּפְנֵי
אֱלוֹהַּ יַעֲקֹב: הַהֹפְכִי הַצּוּר אֲגַם־מָיִם. חַלָּמִישׁ לְמַעְיְנוֹ־מָיִם:

When Israel went out of Egypt,
the house of Yaakov from a people
of a foreign tongue; Yehudah
became His only one, Israel
His Kingdom. The (Red) Sea saw
and fled, the Jordan (River) turned
back. The mountains danced
like rams, the hills like lambs.
What ails you, Sea, that you flee?
the Jordan, that you turn back?
(the) mountains, that you dance
like rams; you hills like lambs?
Tremble, earth, before the Master,
before the God of Yaakov.
He Who turns the rock into
a pool of water, the bedrock
into a flowing spring. (Psalms 114).

THE MATZOT ARE COVERED
AND THE CUP IS HELD.

Blessed are You, God, King
of the universe, Who redeemed
us and redeemed our fathers
from Egypt and brought us
to this night, on which
we eat matzah and maror.
God, God of our fathers:
bring us to celebrate
future festivals and holidays,
may they come to us in peace.
Let us be happy in the rebuilding
of Your city and joyful in Your
service; and there we shall eat
the sacrifices and Pesach
offerings (on Saturday nights
say: the Pesach offerings and
sacrifices), whose blood will be
sprinkled upon the sides
of Your altar for acceptance.
We shall then thank You with a
New Song for our redemption
and for the deliverance of our
souls. Blessed are You, God,
Who has redeemed Israel!

בָּרוּךְ אַתָּה יְיָ, אֱלֹהֵינוּ מֶלֶךְ
הָעוֹלָם אֲשֶׁר גְּאָלָנוּ וְגָאַל אֶת־
אֲבוֹתֵינוּ מִמִּצְרַיִם וְהִגִּיעָנוּ
לַלַּיְלָה הַזֶּה לֶאֱכָל בּוֹ מַצָּה
וּמָרוֹר: כֵּן יְיָ אֱלֹהֵינוּ וֵאלֹהֵי
אֲבוֹתֵינוּ יַגִּיעֵנוּ לְמוֹעֲדִים
וְלִרְגָלִים אֲחֵרִים הַבָּאִים
לִקְרָאתֵנוּ לְשָׁלוֹם שְׂמֵחִים
בְּבִנְיַן עִירֶךָ וְשָׂשִׂים בַּעֲבוֹדָתֶךָ.
וְנֹאכַל שָׁם מִן הַזְּבָחִים וּמִן
הַפְּסָחִים אֲשֶׁר יַגִּיעַ דָּמָם עַל
קִיר מִזְבַּחֲךָ לְרָצוֹן. וְנוֹדֶה לְךָ
שִׁיר חָדָשׁ עַל גְּאֻלָּתֵנוּ וְעַל
פְּדוּת נַפְשֵׁנוּ. בָּרוּךְ אַתָּה יְיָ
גָּאַל יִשְׂרָאֵל:

THE BLESSING OVER
THE SECOND CUP OF WINE IS RECITED:

Blessed are you, God,
King of the universe,
Who created
the fruit of the vine.

בָּרוּךְ אַתָּה יי אֱלֹהֵינוּ מֶלֶךְ
הָעוֹלָם בּוֹרֵא פְּרִי הַגָּפֶן:

THE SECOND CUP OF WINE IS THEN DRUNK
WHILE LEANING TO THE LEFT SIDE.

MAGGID

telling the story of the Exodus from Egypt

AN INVITATION TO INTERPRET

"Maggid" means, "he tells." Maggid is the most important part, at least qualitatively, of the Haggadah. It is the account of the Exodus from Egypt, an anthology compiled from texts chosen by the Sages of the Talmud.

Maggid is preceded by the breaking of Yachatz. The words of the telling emerge from that break, from the empty place left between the two pieces of matzah. That breaking is an invitation to the reader to enter the text to say his own word there. That is why the following part is called maggid, "he tells," rather than "the account." The two pieces of matzah indicate that there must be two in order for the text to exist—the author and the reader. The reader of the Haggadah is not merely the keeper of the text, but also its co-author. The break thus comes to draw the readers out of passivity to make them enter the play of writing, to give them access to the enchantments of writing. The reader is not the dazzled or bored spectator of a story made elsewhere, with which he or she has only distant a relationship. The text speaks to us, about us, and about our own history.

This duality thus becomes that of the text and its commentary. To read is always to comment.

HERE IS THE BREAD

The account of the Haggadah begins with an invitation addressed to anyone who is hungry. Anyone who is hungry may come and celebrate Passover with us. Liberty begins through an invitation to share one's bread. It is not a question of liberating oneself, but of discovering liberty face-to-face with another person. Liberty begins with ethics.

This face-to-face is already included in the very word "maggid," for it comes from the root "nagad," which means "to oppose," "to be against," "to be opposite." This is the word we can use when we are in the presence of an object or a person and can point to them with our finger because they are present, facing us.

This is also seen in the famous phrase, "And God said, 'It is not good that man be alone. I will make him a helper, kenegdo'" (Genesis 2:18), meaning that woman was created as a face-to-face creature, a creature of dialogue, as opposed to the primordial form of the original androgyne, where male and female were back to back.

This meaning of the maggid as a word that one may accompany with a gesture of the hand to show what one is talking about is very much present in the Haggadah, which unfolds around the Seder Plate, and around several concrete objects that one shows to all assembled every time one refers to them in the account.

The first word of the maggid is indeed "Here," and while speaking the words, "ha lachma anya," "here is the bread of affliction," the head of the family or the one leading the Seder shows the matzah to the guests!

TO THINK IS FIRST OF ALL TO QUESTION

After the invitation to share the bread, the actual account begins with a series of questions that bring out the changes introduced by the Seder ritual.

Thought, and thinking, are the ascent of affirmation toward questioning: "I ask questions, thus I exist."

That is the interrogative credo proposed by the Haggadah.

Beyond affirmation and negation, there is the interrogation in which human transcendence is revealed.

The Haggadah begins with astonishment: "Ma nishtana?"—"What has changed?" "How is this night different from other nights?"

Astonishment does not consist in being astonished by what is astonishing. Such a situation is not astonishing at all. True astonishment consists in being astonished by something that is not astonishing.

One must render astonishing things that are peaceful, simple, understandable, habitual, commonly accepted, and shared by everyone.

Astonishment must be directed at everything that is around us: time, space, things, people like us, animals, plants, tools, etc., and ourselves.

The question is not directed at the unknown, at mysterious and invisible worlds, distant and difficult of access, but at what is near, the nearby, everything that is in our proximity, and that we encounter first of all.

Why?

"Because what we encounter first of all is not what is near but always what is habitual. Now, that which is habitual properly possesses the frightening power to make us unused to it and to dwell in the essential, and often in a manner so decisive that it never allows us to manage to dwell there." (Translated from Martin Heidegger, Qu'appelle-t-on penser?, PUF, 1959).

By astonishment and questioning, a person will be able to liberate himself once and for all from the grip (which may be unconscious) of certain habits of thought, convictions, theories accepted without verification, opinions, prejudices, ready-made decisions that decree what are the world, things, people, knowledge, etc.

The obligation of questioning has no limit of age or social category. Everyone—children, women, men, Sages, etc.—has the obligation to question.

Customarily, the youngest child present asks the Four Questions. If only a couple are present, the wife asks her husband, and if one is alone, one asks oneself.

The obligation of telling that begins with the Four Questions is also an unavoidable obligation that does not depend upon the knowledge or status of the person. Everyone has the obligation to tell. What is at stake in this telling is the creation of a narrative identity in every participant, reader, or simple listener to the text. Telling involves the status of the human being as a speaking body, as the articulation of a body with its speech, as a possibility of transmitting speech. And as the possibility of transmitting history, the origins of a body that is anchored in speech and desire. This is valid on both the individual and collective levels. The Haggadah is the construction of an account of the Jewish people since their origins. One great discovery of psychoanalysis lies in that intuition of the importance of the story of origins for the structure of a balanced personality.

An individual's future, his name, cannot be constructed without being anchored in all the levels of memory. In particular, one must have access to the time before one could speak, the time when one was infants, a non-speaker, but understanding everything that happened around one, the moment when the others, one's parents, spoke to one another and desired one another, and desired the infant and spoke to it.

Stories participate in this oral tradition where the secret of birth and death is spoken in a hidden word that only the unconscious can hear. The disappearance of a myth, or merely the impoverishment of its tradition, signifies not only social disorganization of the bond between people, in their work and in their heads, but mainly a veritable ontological deracination and the jarring of the world's tectonic plates.

For the child, to receive the word of a story is to make it communicate with speech that gives it foundations in myth. The story, like the myth, contains the inexplicable secret of knowledge that defies and forbids memory and where one finds what one needs to know who one is and how one is. In a word, the story is what inscribes one genealogically in the world order and in one's identity. That is the very significance of the Haggadah.

THE FOUR QUESTIONS

In this part of the maggid, the Haggadah presents the four sons. Each one, in his own way, asks a question. Even the one who does not know how to ask is taught how to do so. What is the meaning of placing the question on stage?

In human relations, the important thing is truly to encounter the thou as a thou. That means not to be deaf to his appeal, but to enable one to have something said to one by him. This demands openness. Whoever places himself in the position of listening is fundamentally open. Without this openness between one another, there is no authentic human tie. To be tied to another means always knowing how to listen to one another. To be open to the other thus implies that I accept the affirmation within me of something that is contrary to me, even when there is no adversary who maintains something against me. We call the posing of a question false if it does not touch that openness, but rather prevents access to it. The art of questioning is thus the art of continuing to question, hence the art of thinking.

The first dimension of the question is openness to the other.

Taking the other's speech seriously implies a proper response, truly oriented toward the other. The recounting should not be a text indifferent to the listeners' preoccupations, but rather a response to personal and existential questions. To tell is first of all to make certain that a question is asked. Thus to tell is to respond. Thus the story becomes the location of a movement of questions and replies.

Within the horizon of the problematic status of history, it may also be said that one cannot truly understand a text without having understood the question to which it is an answer.

THE TEN PLAGUES: A REFLECTION ON THE JEWISH PHILOSOPHY OF HISTORY

The Haggadah, and particularly the section called "maggid," is actually a synthetic text that brings together passages taken from the Bible, Midrash, the Talmud, and the liturgy, all combined as a narrative that recapitulates the history of the Jewish people, especially emphasizing the founding event: the period of slavery in Egypt and the Exodus from Egypt. The most interesting point is that one finds not only the historical account but also, quite originally, a reflection on the Jewish philosophy of history. Today, no one believes that the work of the historian consists simply in recording a raw fact and reproducing the reality of the past, "just as it happened," as the naive positivists suggested.

At any time one may compose an astonishing diversity of interpretations—some of them antithetical—of any single event. In this interpretive pluralism, no interpretation is rejected, except those resulting from violence or that produce violence. Every commentary, every explanation, is transformed into one hypothesis among many, one explicative element among a diversity of other possibilities.

In this problematic situation of interpretive pluralism, the following passage from the Haggadah is entirely exemplary:

"These are the Ten Plagues that the Holy One, blessed be He, inflicted upon Egypt: blood, frogs, vermin, wild beasts, plague, boils, hail, locusts, darkness, and the slaying of the firstborn."

Rabbi Yehuda offers a mnemonic: "d'tzach, adash, b'achav"

Rabbi Yose the Galilean says: "How do we know that the Egyptians suffered from ten plagues on the land and fifty plagues on the sea?"

What game are these Talmudists playing with our text here?

Regarding a real historical event that took place fifteen centuries before their discussion, they propose three different versions, beginning with the same kernel of reality—that of the biblical text, which all three accept as a common horizon.

These different ways of understanding the event are not based on intuition, but on interpretation of the text.

The historical account is not the product of perception, but of a hermeneutic (interpretive) situation. Thus the historical account is not the presentation of what happened. It is a work of language, a narrative artifice that constructs what was done.

Every work of history is merely an interpretation of history. Hence it is necessary to avoid enclosing oneself within a monist vision that seeks to explain everything. Instead, each time one must develop the ensemble of possibilities in the interpretive field.

The playful character of the text of the Haggadah does not detract from the serious character of the problematic situation that is brought to light. The identical verse cited by all three authors contains a unique event, a plurality of interpretations.

The fabrication of History is also the fabrication of memory. It retains certain elements, certain aspects of the events that took place, and rejects or passes over other aspects in silence, which is even more effective.

Within the framework of our text, none of the Sages who speak desires to falsify reality. First of all, there were the ten plagues—everyone agrees on the material to be analyzed. The rest is merely interpretation. If it is true that the interpretations are infinite, the text is there as a foundation upon which the Talmudic Sages agree in order to join the dance of meaning.

MITECHILA: TOWARD A PEDAGOGY THROUGH EXILE

The Haggadah tells a story, but what story? What logic does the Haggadah wish to teach us? What model of the chain of causality must we retain?

Before the Revelation on Mount Sinai, before the Ten Commandments, a fundamental word was addressed to Abraham, the founder of monotheism. The word came before the law, the word that established history: "Lech-lecha,"—"Go away from your country, from your homeland, from the house of your father, to the land that I shall show you." The first revelation consists in a message of uprooting.

THE NOTION OF EXILE IS PART OF THE DIVINE PLAN

God said to Abraham, "Know that your seed will be a stranger in a land not their own, and they shall serve them; and they shall afflict them four hundred years."

As surprising as this may seem, God is the one who makes the decision to send the descendants of Abraham into exile as though it were an ontological necessity of the human condition, as though it were the best historical option for humanity.

Exile precedes history, the very possibility of history!

The connection between the Jew and exile is thus no accident!

A NECESSARY DETOUR

Let us present an anecdote, a sort of contemporary midrash, which appears to us to be paradigmatic.

When Yitzhak Goren, an Israeli author, published his novel An Alexandrian Summer, which tells the story of Jewish families in Egypt, he changed his name back to Gormezano, the name he had when he arrived in Israel during the 1950s. His new immigrant parents had taken the Hebrew name of Goren. Within the tiny territory of the name Gormezano, he finds traces of centuries of wandering.

Here is his story:

"Gormezano is the name that was given to my ancestors upon their arrival in Spain before the Inquisition, because they came from Gorms, which is to say, Worms, a German city, where they were persecuted and from which they were driven. Thus, during the Middle Ages, these German Jews from Worms arrived in Spain, which was the America of its day. They lived there for a while, but their name and their history came from elsewhere, from Gorms.

"So in Spain we had the merit of a half-German, half-Spanish name, the mixture of two Diasporas in a single name, which created in advance an obstacle to any possibility of integration.

"Actually, my ancestors did not remain in Spain. The Expulsion of the Jews of Spain in 1492 put them on the road of wandering again. They went northward, as far as Sweden, where they did not give up the name Gormezano. For their part, the Swedes took them for Spaniards. For the Swedes, this insistence on their origins concealed the refusal to allow these foreigners to become natives. While for the Gormezanos, the use of a name that came from elsewhere indicated attachment to that other place. Later my ancestors went from Sweden to Turkey. There they were known as 'Suedos.' From Turkey they reached Egypt and became 'Turquanos.' Finally, when they reached Israel, they were known as Egyptians, Egyptians named Gormezano, referring to the German city of Worms, which they had left so long ago.

"That was when my parents felt the need to adapt their name to the Israeli language and Hebraize it as Goren.

"But I have returned to Gormezano, because that means that my name reflects my history."

He adds:

"Over the generations, my parents were surnamed in all sorts of ways, always as a function of the places they had left behind. They never had the privilege of being identified with the place where they were actually living.

In Israel, a certain sense of exile dwells within me. I needed a departure from Israel for America, that is to say a passage through exile in the Diaspora, to rid myself of that sentiment, of the malaise that dwelled within me. Then I returned from America, I had worked through my relation with exile, though it remained complex.

We are a restless people, of beneficial diversity, and only the acceptance of that dynamic existence there will allow us to develop here a culture that will be both specific and universal.

"It is only by facing the exilic dimension within us that we will perhaps succeed in finding an authentic and profound new identity." (Quoted by B. D. Hercenberg, translated from L'exil et la puissance d'Israël et du monde, Actes Sud (1990), pp. 194)

One might ask whether that notion of exile does not contradict the notion of the Temple and of a central place for the cult as instituted in the Biblical text.

The Talmud provokes a revolution in mentalities that always felt the psychological temptation of stability and the feeling of security that comes from enclosure within borders.

The Temple is not a goal in itself. Immediately after the revelation on Mount Sinai, the Bible says, "You shall make an altar of earth for Me... in all places where I record my name, I will come unto you, and I will bless you." (Exodus 20:24)

The text goes on to say, "And if you make Me an altar of stone, you shall not build it of hewn stone, for if you raise your sword against it, it is profane."

The Divine Presence is everywhere!

The verse we have just quoted is important, because it sets limits to the religious sphere.

If the sword touches the stones, the meeting place between human beings and God is profaned!

The theological meeting place cannot be constructed by violence, and in no case may it lead to violence.

The idea that the divine service is possible in any location is reinforced by the construction of the desert sanctuary, the Mishkan, the place that will receive the Shechina, the Divine Presence.

This sanctuary is a large, portable tent that is erected and dismantled during the journeys of the Israelites in the desert.

The center of the Mishkan is the Holy Ark, made of wood and gold and containing the first and second tablets of the Law, as well as a copy of the Five Books of Moses, the Torah.

This Holy Ark is carried on staves that must never be removed, even when the Ark has reached its final destination: the Temple of Solomon.

The Sages of the Talmud ask the reason for this prohibition.

The answer is very simple: the Holy Ark never ceases travelling.

Sanctity is an infinite journey. Mankind is not. Mankind becomes.

THE TALMUD: A TEMPLE OF PAPER

Let us recall the destruction of the Second Temple. It is the year 70 C.E. The Roman army, led by Vespasian, has encircled Jerusalem. The Jews resist fiercely, but hunger and illness have begun to weaken them seriously. One of the important rabbis of the city, Rabbi ben Zakai, understanding that the military battle is lost, plans to risk everything by speaking directly to Vespasian. To leave the besieged city, he uses a stratagem. He has his illness and then his death proclaimed, has himself placed in a coffin, and his disciples carry him out of the walls. He reaches Vespasian, and when he is allowed to speak to him, he says: "Greetings, Emperor."

Vespasian, who is merely a general, is surprised by this form of address and is planning to punish the insolent man who has accorded him an untimely rank. At that very moment a messenger arrives from Rome and cries out, "Long live the emperor!"

Vespasian turns to Rabbi Yochanan and says, "To reward you for being the first to call me emperor, ask me what you want, and I will grant it."

Rabbi Yochanan, who could have demanded the end of the siege and the abandonment of the plan to destroy the Temple, makes a request that seems strange at first, but which is one of the most important mental revolutions in Jewish history. "I want," he says, "permission for several disciples and myself to establish a Talmudic academy in the small city of Yavne." Nonplussed, Vespasian accepts immediately. This episode seals the birth certificate of modern Judaism.

Despite the infinite loss of the stone Temple built by King Solomon, a new Temple was being born, that of the spirit and of study, thanks to which the Jewish people would be able to live through history, exiles, and the most horrible suffering.

A new Temple was born, an invisible edifice, as Freud said so beautifully. It is an invisible edifice that is constructed year after year, century after century, in the thousands of pages that today constitute the Mishnah, the Gemara, the Talmud, and its infinite commentaries.

The new space of sanctity is the Book!

The new space of sanctity is study!

Part Six

RACHATZAH

RACHATZAH

washing and purifying the hands

WASH THE HANDS AND RECITE THE BLESSING.

בָּרוּךְ אַתָּה יְיָ אֱלֹהֵינוּ מֶלֶךְ
הָעוֹלָם אֲשֶׁר קִדְּשָׁנוּ בְּמִצְוֹתָיו
וְצִוָּנוּ עַל נְטִילַת יָדִים:

Blessed are You, God,
King of the universe,
Who has made us holy with His mitzvot,
and commanded us to wash the hands.

ONE SHOULD NOT TALK UNTIL AFTER EATING
THE MATZAH (PREFERABLY THAT OF THE KORECH).

RACHATZAH

washing and purifying the hands

This sixth part of the Seder consists in washing and purifying the hands. The participants in the Seder take the keli (the vessel), fill it with water, and pour water on their hands. Customarily, one first pours water three times on the right hand and then three times on the left. The blessing for this ritual speaks of raising the hands, "netilat yadayim."

The purpose of this gesture is not to clean the hands but to purify them. Even if one's hands are clean, one must pour the water in order to be aware of two things: connection and transmission. "See to it not only that we leave Egypt, but also that Egypt leaves us!" (Translated from Armand Abécassis, Les temps du partage, *Albin Michel, 1992.)*

TO TRANSMIT AND TO GIVE

At the time of the revelation on Mount Sinai, the Torah was written on stone tablets.

Why stone?

In Hebrew, the words for "stone tablets" are "luchot avanim." "Evven" is stone. This word can be divided in two, as "av" and "ben," meaning "father" and "son." Thus the word for stone signifies the genealogical link between parent and child. That is to say, it is a link between generations. Giving the Torah on stone tablets thus signifies that the essence of its inscription is not a static matter of stone, but a generational dynamic of transmission.

JUDAISM: THE POWER OF TRANSMISSION

Historical and archaeological discoveries permit us to note many close resemblances between the Torah and legislative and narrative texts of the same region and epoch. One may note, for example, the texts of Ras-Shamra and the famous Code of Hammurabi.

Without any apologetic intent, we may nevertheless note that the difference between the Torah and these other texts is that the Torah has come to us whole and constantly enriched, while the other texts are mere vestiges, the ruins of thought and civilization, the remains that archaeology and history offer us.

This remark underscores the following fundamental idea: the power of the biblical text is perhaps not only in its content, but in its ability to be transmitted by a people from generation to generation. The key word in the biblical text is perhaps the word "transmission." It is no

coincidence that Moses is traditionally called "Moshe Rabenu," "Moses our master."

This is also the meaning of the Hebrew word for Hebrew, "ivri," which comes from the same root as "laavor," "to pass," and "lehaavir," "to transmit."

THE TRANSMISSION OF LIGHT AND ENERGY IN THE KABBALAH

After a first phase called "Tsimtsum," which corresponds to God's retreat from the infinite to leave room for the world and for humanity, light penetrates the empty space in the form of energy-light. It becomes material in the form of ten vessels, which the Kabbalah called "Sefirot," and which will receive and contain the light. The light that created them fills them one after the other.

Each Sefira is both masculine and feminine. It is feminine in that it receives and masculine when it gives. The light of the luminous ray reaches the first Sefira, which, once it is filled, transmits the remaining light to the following Sefira.

Light, having thus entered in the form of a ray, will be at the origin of the creations of worlds and the forces at work in life and creation.

When a Sefira receives light, is filled with it, but does not transmit it to the following Sefirot, the energy-light contained in the Sefira becomes so strong that it explodes. This is the episode known in Kabbalah as "the smashing of the vessels."

LIFE: RECEIVING AND GIVING

What is the existential, concrete meaning of the great world allegory deployed by Kabbalah? The commentators have suggested that we look at the map of Israel.

On the map, the Mediterranean is on the left, and, on the right, the Jordan river descends from the north to the south and empties into a lake, the Sea of Galilee. It then flows further south until it reaches the Dead Sea.

The Kabbalists asked themselves why give it the name "Dead Sea"? What definition can be given of something that is dead?

The answer is both of extraordinary simplicity and also of formidable import. The Sea of Galilee is the lake of life, because it receives the Jordan, is filled with its water, and liberates it further to the south. It receives and it gives.

In contrast, the Dead Sea receives water from the Jordan, takes it, but does not give anything back.

Here is a very concrete definition of death: that which is capable of receiving but not of giving in return. And to receive without giving in return corresponds precisely to what the Kabbalists call "the smashing of the vessels."

PURIFICATION OF THE HANDS: NETILAT YADAYIM OR RACHATZAH

This idea of receiving-giving is found in every area of life and, in particular, in the ritual of nourishing oneself.

For the Kabbalists, the table ritual is fundamental. To eat is to draw forces and to set in motion the dynamic of the sparks of sanctity. Eating is a Kabbalistic rite that consists in performing a "tikkun," a reparation of the broken vessels. The tikkun is accomplished by purifying one's hands and by sharing bread.

The purification of one's hands and the blessing at the time of the meal are viewed from the same perspective. Let us recall this ritual. Before eating bread, one washes one's hands from a vessel, not directly from a faucet. One pours water into the vessel and empties it onto one's hands, the way the Sea of Galilee fills with water from the Jordan and later gives it up. This ritual is called "netilat yadayim," "raising the hands," which are thus purified. Moreover, one learns that this ritual of purity is an ethical idea that is properly translated by receiving-giving, that is to say, by transmission and sharing!

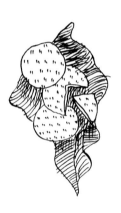

Part Seven

MOTZI-MATZAH

מוֹצִיא מַצָּה

MOTZI-MATZAH

sharing and eating the unleavened bread

HOLD ALL THREE MATZOT, AND RECITE:

בָּרוּךְ אַתָּה יְיָ אֱלֹהֵינוּ מֶלֶךְ
הָעוֹלָם הַמּוֹצִיא לֶחֶם מִן הָאָרֶץ:

Blessed are You, God, King of the universe,
Who brings forth bread from the earth.

AFTER RETURNING THE BOTTOM MATZAH
TO THE SEDER PLATE, RAISE THE TOP
AND MIDDLE MATZOT (BEARING IN MIND
THAT THE BLESSING SHALL ALSO APPLY
TO THE MATZAH OF THE KORECH
AND AFIKOMAN) AND RECITE:

בָּרוּךְ אַתָּה יְיָ אֱלֹהֵינוּ מֶלֶךְ
הָעוֹלָם אֲשֶׁר קִדְּשָׁנוּ בְּמִצְוֹתָיו
וְצִוָּנוּ עַל אֲכִילַת מַצָּה:

Blessed are You, God,
King of the universe,
Who has made us holy
with His mitzvot,
and commanded us
to eat matzah.

מוֹצִיא מַצָּה

MOTZI-MATZAH

sharing and eating the unleavened bread

TWO BENEDICTIONS

This seventh part of the Seder consists of two benedictions. The first one is the classic benediction recited every time one eats bread, called "Hamotzi," meaning, "Who brings out." The central expression in the blessing says that we thank God for bringing bread from the earth. Gratitude and thanks are offered to the earth for its fertility. The second blessing is for matzah.

Matzah is unleavened bread. The Haggadah plays here on the similarity of sound between "motzi" and "matzah." Though they come from different roots, the similarity in sound lets one hear "motzi" in the matzah ritual. Matzah is meant to remind us that God brought the children of Israel out of Egypt, just as He brings bread from the earth.

THE GUEST: LIGHT AND FRAGRANCE

Before one can eat, according to the tradition one must see that the domestic animals have received food, and must also, break the bread, even if one eats alone. This day-to-day ethic conveys extraordinary symbolism: I can never begin to eat without making a gesture that signifies that I am prepared to share my bread with someone else. This is a humanism of the other person, to quote a fine expression of Emmanuel Levinas. (In L'humanisme de l'autre homme, Fata Morgana, 1972.)

This gesture is the culmination of the meaning of the Haggadah, which began with the invitation to the other person to come and share one's bread: "Here is the bread of affliction, whoever is hungry may come and eat!"

The Hebrew word for guest is "orayach," a very beautiful word from the same root as the word for a path, "orach." We can also read the word as "or" and "rayach", meaning "light" and "fragrance."

Everyone with whom we share bread, even our relatives, is regarded as a guest.

The gesture of sharing gives the status of guest to another person. Thus, to share bread is to open one's house to the light and fragrance of life. By welcoming another person, one becomes oneself, welcomed by the other, welcomed by light and fragrance.

THE MATZAH IS BROKEN

The gesture of breaking bread is one of the most essential gestures of Judaism. Since on Pesach it is forbidden to eat any bread or other food containing leavening, this blessing is made for matzah, unleavened bread.

What does this gesture mean?

That a person is always engaged already in a relationship with another human being. "To be is to be with." The relationship is not another prerogative of humanity. Rather it constitutes humanity ontologically. As the verse in Genesis states, "It is not good for man to be alone; I will make him a helpmate."

Sharing bread is a symbol of friendship and love.

THE JOY OF SHARING

To love is the art of knowing how to give and share. Love consists essentially in giving, not in receiving. Giving is the source of more joy than receiving, because one's vitality is expressed in the gift. It constitutes the highest expression of power. In the very act of giving, I feel myself as superabundant, spending, living, free, and hence joyful. The Talmud teaches: "eizehu ashir? ha'samayach bechelko." This is generally translated as, "who is rich? the one who is happy with his share." Shlomo Rotnemer has suggested another possible translation: "who is rich? the one who is happy in sharing."

In the sphere of material relations, giving signifies that one is rich—not that the man who has a lot is rich, but that the man who gives a lot is rich. The miser who anxiously tortures himself with the thought of losing something is, psychologically speaking, a poor man, impoverished, even though he may be wealthy. People capable of giving of themselves are rich.

THE SHARING OF BREAD AND THE DEW OF RESURRECTION

Traditional commentaries use an interesting and fertile interpretative procedure known as Gematria. Gematria is a calculation of the numerical value of Hebrew letters and words. It is one of the thirty-two hermeneutic rules transmitted by Rabbi Yose Hagalili at the end of Brachot, a treatise of the Talmud. Gematria is the twenty-ninth of these rules, in the category of "halacha le'moshe mi'sinai" (a law transmitted orally to Moses on Mount Sinai). Thus it is an integral part of Oral Law.

The numerical value of the word "lechem" ("bread") is 78.

Lamed = 30; Chet = 8; Mem = 40.

If we take the expression "sharing bread" literally, we can divide the numerical value of the word for bread in two, obtaining the number 39, which corresponds to the word "tal," which means "dew."

To offer a piece of bread is to offer a few drops of dew.

According to the prophetic tradition, dew is the sign of resurrection, as is said in Isaiah 26:19: "Awake and sing, you who lie in the earth, because your dew is 39 lights."

To offer bread goes beyond the act of offering the energy of subsistence to another person; it is to offer the power of resurrection.

Go, rise up! Or, Rise up and go!

It is offering that which allows the other to go beyond himself. "We offer them knowledge of their limits, but also the ability to experiment, to know, and to discover what other geographies look like, places where they had not expected to venture, to learn to go beyond their certitudes in order to plunge a bit into the nights that border upon souls." (Translated from Michel Onfray, Les vertus de la foudre, *p. 248).*

TO OFFER A SMILE

Nevertheless, the most important sphere of giving is not in material things but in the specifically human domain. What does one being give to another? One gives oneself, that which is most precious. One gives one's life. This does not necessarily mean that one sacrifices one's life for the other, but that one gives that which is most alive within one. One gives one's joy, one's interest, one's comprehension, one's knowledge, one's humor, one's sadness—in short, everything that expresses and manifests what lives within one. In thus giving one's life, one enriches the other. One raises the receiver's sense of vitality at the same time as one raises one's own.

The Talmud presents a teaching of great beauty on this matter. At the end of Jacob's blessing to Judah, we find a sentence that can be translated: "His eyes are darker than wine; his teeth are whiter than milk" (Gen. 49:12). The commentators had great difficulty in finding a satisfactory explanation of this verse, until Rav Dimmi taught:

"The Congregation of Israel said to God: Master of the universe, make us a sign with your eyes, this is better than wine, and show your teeth [in a smile], this is better than milk."

That teaching can be understood thanks to a further explanation found in the teachings of Rabbi Yochanan:

"The whiteness of one's teeth [in a smile] that one offers to one's friend is better than a good bowl of milk."

In his commentary, Rashi finalizes this teaching by saying that in the human face there is a smile of eyes and a smile of the mouth, an upper smile and a lower smile. This is also how one must understand Jacob's blessing of Judah:

"Do not forget that the smile of the eyes is preferable to the best of wines, and that the smile of the mouth is preferable to the most comforting cup of milk."

Part Eight

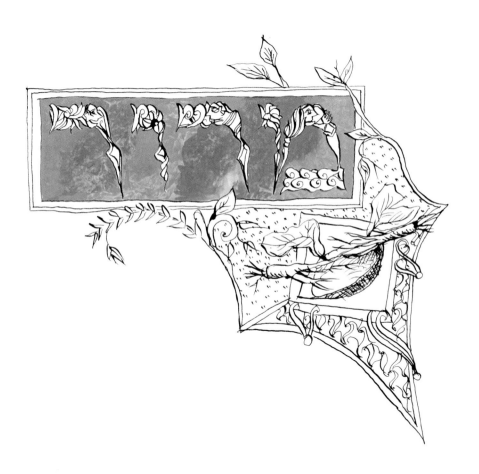

MAROR

MAROR

eating the bitter herbs

DIP THE MAROR IN THE CHAROSET

AND RECITE THE FOLLOWING:

בָּרוּךְ אַתָּה יְיָ אֱלֹהֵינוּ מֶלֶךְ
הָעוֹלָם אֲשֶׁר קִדְּשָׁנוּ בְּמִצְוֹתָיו
וְצִוָּנוּ עַל אֲכִילַת מָרוֹר:

Blessed are You, God, King of the universe,
Who has made us holy with His mitzvot,
and commanded us to eat maror.

THEN EAT THE MAROR WITHOUT RECLINING.

JOSEPH IN THE PIT (GENESIS 37:22)

MAROR

eating the bitter herbs

"Im ata maamin she'ata yachol lekalkel, taamin she'gam ata yachol le'takain."
("If you believe that you can destroy, also believe that you can rebuild.")
Rabbi Nachman of Bratslav

DESCENT AND ASCENT

The eighth part of the Seder consists in eating the bitter herbs, the maror. In the account of the maggid, the fifth section, we mentioned the obligation to proclaim the three key words of the Seder: "Any person who has not pronounced these three words on Pesach has not fulfilled his ritual obligations."

PESACH, MATZAH, MAROR

That is to say, anyone who has not tried to understand and comment on the meaning of these three words has not fully explored the meaning of the Passover holiday.

Pesach is the paschal sacrifice that our ancestors ate during the Exodus from Egypt, and they still ate when the Temple stood. (See our commentary on Shulchan Orech and the question of blood.)

Matzah is the unleavened bread that our ancestors ate.

Maror is the bitter herb. This is an allusion to the forced labor and slavery of Egypt.

IT IS FORBIDDEN TO DESPAIR!

We have insisted on presenting these texts because they are the scriptural basis of the Haggadah, and they also allow us to better understand the historical horizon of the Haggadah. Moreover, the order in which they are cited by the Haggadah is already a commentary in itself! In effect, the historical logic is as follows: descent into Egypt, the suffering and bitterness of slavery (maror), the Exodus from Egypt, symbolized by the lamb (pesach) and the unleavened bread (matzah). Hence the ritual formula of the Seder ought to have been maror, pesach, matzah. Why did the formula taught by Rabban Gamliel make the Exodus from Egypt precede slavery? There are two possible answers. The first consists in emphasizing that comprehension of the Passover Haggadah makes the causal and linear logic of before and after questionable, because liberty proceeds from another logic, which is neither linear nor causal.

The second answer is the fundamental lesson of the Haggadah: in the ontological and cosmic order, redemption precedes the fall. The ascent is always already a possibility before the descent. If there is a descent, it is to rise again, "yerida le'tzorech haaliya!" This is what Rabbi Nachman of Bratslav teaches when he proclaims: "It is forbidden to despair!"

A FUNDAMENTAL OPTIMISM

Ba'al-Haorot, the Master of Lights teaches:

"There is a light that circulates and crosses all the worlds, from the smallest atom to beyond the greatest galaxies. This is the fundamental energy of every living thing. The flux and reflux of every organism.

"Once the world was created, it entered into a process of rising up to its source again, and it constructs itself, from bottom to top, from the least perfect to the more perfect.

"There is a 'tension toward perfection.' The world rises more and more and constantly acquires new goods, adding them to the first, and organizing them in entities full of force and spendlor." (Translated from Ba'al-Haorot, Orot haqodech, Mossad Harav Kook, 1975.)

"Reality progresses, renews itself, is always better and always higher, approaching the Light of the Infinite.

"The process of elevation is infinite, because it lays bare the force of the divine will in the universe, a force that aspires to absolute good. The evolution of the world is a positive process and the foundation of optimism in the world. For how could one despair when one sees that everything develops and rises?" (Ba'al-Haorot, p. 537)

The evolution of creation toward something ever Higher is the source of the fundamental optimism of Jewish thought.

This infinite yearning for something more profound, "better," "higher," is the very sense of messianism, faith in the perfection of humanity in its return toward the infinite, the source of all life...

The essence of being is time, which in the human realm is translated by the dynamic force that infinitely renews and perfects the world.

"Everything comes and ascends. Every action is an ascent. Even descents, within their interior, are ascents. Everything comes, flows, and rises.... Every true poet, every person who knows how to penetrate the innerness of things, every person who heeds the spirit of sanctity, perceives all of reality in its dynamic elevation... A person must feel the world not as something complete and finished, but as something always in the process of becoming, of rising, of developing, and that must develop further. Everything renews itself. That is what we call 'hachidush hatemidi.'

"In every little part of the world, in every instant, even the tiniest parcel of being is in motion, attracted or repelled, repelled and attracted, rising, falling, always rising even when its exterior aspect is one of descent, coming and going infinitely, according to the words of the prophet Ezekiel: 'and the creatures came and went' ('vehachayot ratso veshov'), an expression that can also be read, 'vehachayut ratso veshov,' meaning, 'cosmic vitality is always in the process of coming and going.'

"Even the smallest parcel of being contains a spark of sanctity that aspires to return to its sources and that produces a fundamental movement of elevation and of the dynamics of existence.

"The ascents and descents are uninterrupted in people and in the entire cosmos. Every movement, even a fall, a descent, or a psychological depression is an elevation. Changes of state, of mood, and even deep depressions have a positive value.

"It is the moon, almost invisible before its renewal. It is the low tide before the return of high tide. It is sleep, that provides rebirth and strength for being aroused and awakened....

"A fall is not an accident but a natural movement of our inscription in the world.

"Did the world not issue from the descent of the infinite light?

According to a famous expression regarding the matzah, there is a state of 'yerida le'tzorech haaliya,' a descent that can have no outcome except ascent." (Following Orot hakodesh, Vol. II, 1978, fifth discourse, pp. 511)

BREAD AND TIME

The preceding comments also allow us to deepen the meaning of matzah. Historically, the matzah was bread that had not had time to rise during the Exodus from Egypt. From a ritual point of view, the problem is to bake bread that does not rise. Interestingly, on boxes of matzah sold today one can find the expression, "Eighteen Minute Matzah." That means that from the beginning of the making of the matzah until they are baked, eighteen minutes have not elapsed.

The essential difference between bread and matzah is time!

Bread is an object that contains time: the time necessary for fermentation; the time for the dough to rise. Anyone who has baked bread knows the expression, "letting the dough rest."

The danger of bread is the time that could become pure passivity. One lets things happen without thinking that they can change, without thinking that one can begin something new.

Matzah is a bread without time that says precisely that we must not fall into the trap of passing time. If you leave bread out too long, it becomes stale and inedible. Matzah, one might say, grows old less slowly!

The difference between bread and matzah would be the one we can make between culture and barbarism in the following sense:

What is culture? Every culture is a culture of life, an action that life performs upon itself, by which it transforms itself. "Culture" designates none other than the self-transformation of life, the movement by which it never ceases modifying itself, in order to reach higher forms of achievement and accomplishment, to grow, to transform itself, and to fulfill itself.

A culture that does not continue this movement of creation, elevation, and perfection, even if it can regard itself as having reached a very high level, enters the universe of barbarism. A culture that does not renew itself is a barbaric culture.

Matzah is spiritual vigilance to avoid falling into the trap of cultural self-satisfaction, on the individual or the collective level.

Matzah is a reminder of the power of life that exists in everything and that endlessly seeks to act, to create, and to invent. Even when the elementary forms of life seem to be frozen, and their blind transmission results in the simple reproduction of indefinitely repeated structures, matzah allows us to perceive that, at the world's deepest level of being, profound forces are at work and can still blossom. One then sees that these hidden forces, as though dormant, "do not merely maintain the state of affairs that permits the continuation of life, but that they remain on watch and that, not satisfied with preserving that which is, they await, with patience measured in the millennia they have traversed, the opportunity of finding a foothold in the acquired past in order to take a leap, to discover as yet unnoticed connections, to invent a tool, an idea, to make a new world arise." (Translated from Michel Henry, La barbarie, Grasset, 1987, pp. 13, 14.)

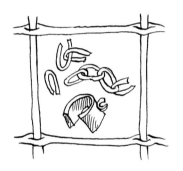

Part Nine

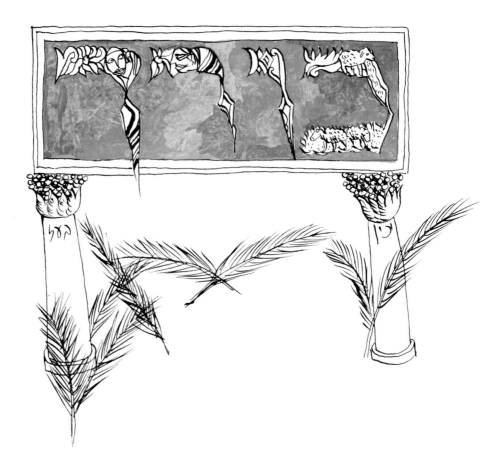

KORECH

כּוֹרֵךְ

KORECH

performing the ritual initiated by Hillel

TAKE THE BOTTOM MATZAH,

PUT MAROR ON IT,

AND RECITE THE FOLLOWING PASSAGE:

זֵכֶר לְמִקְדָּשׁ כְּהִלֵּל:
כֵּן עָשָׂה הִלֵּל בִּזְמַן שֶׁבֵּית הַמִּקְדָּשׁ הָיָה
קַיָּם. הָיָה כּוֹרֵךְ (פֶּסַח) מַצָּה וּמָרוֹר וְאוֹכֵל
בְּיַחַד. לְקַיֵּם מַה שֶּׁנֶּאֱמַר. עַל מַצּוֹת
וּמְרֹרִים יֹאכְלֻהוּ:

A commemoration of the Holy Temple, according to Hillel's custom.
This is what Hillel did at the time when the Holy Temple stood:
he would combine (the paschal lamb), matzah and maror, and eat them
together. This, in order to fulfill what is written: "They shall eat it
(the paschal lamb) with matzah and bitter herbs" (Exodus 12:8).

THEN EAT THE MATZAH-MAROR SANDWICH WHILE RECLINING TO THE LEFT.

KORECH

performing the ritual initiated by Hillel

TWO QUESTIONS CONCERNING THE RITE OF HILLEL

After eating matzah and maror separately, we eat them together.

"Korech" means "to bind together."

The Haggadah reports a custom practiced by the Talmudic master Hillel when the Temple in Jerusalem was still the center of the Jewish religion. He ate the three foods symbolic of liberation together—pesach, matzah, and maror—following the biblical prescription, which is repeated twice: "They shall eat the flesh that same night; they shall eat it roasted over the fire, with unleavened bread and bitter herbs." (Exodus 12:8); "They shall eat it with unleavened bread and bitter herbs." (Numbers 9:11)

A fundamental question may be asked here: In what way is Hillel's practice original, since he is carrying out the biblical injunction to the letter? One may add a second question: Since two verses give the commandment, why does the Haggadah cite the one in Numbers, referring to the second Pesach, and not the one in Exodus to justify Hillel's custom?

THE SECOND PESACH: THE AWAKENING BELOW

Hillel is not speaking of the first Passover, which took place precisely during the Exodus from Egypt, but of the second Passover, which was celebrated a year after the Exodus, when Pesach had already become a ritual commemorating an event that had taken place the year before. Thus the tradition distinguishes among four sorts of Pesach. The first took place in Egypt itself, at the moment of the Exodus, and it is known as "Pesach Mitzrayim"–"the Passover of Egypt". The second is the one that the Israelites celebrated in the desert before entering the Land of Israel, and this is known as "Pesach Midbar"–"the Passover of the Desert". The third is all the Passovers that have followed from generation to generation, known as "Pesach Dorot"–"the Passover of Generations". The fourth is the delayed Passover or "Pesach Sheni"–"Second Pesach", celebrated a month after the first one by those who were unable to celebrate Passover at the prescribed time (see Numbers 9:10).

The Second Pesach is of fundamental importance for understanding relations between mankind and the tradition and between mankind and God. The First Passover and that of generations are the experience and commemoration of the liberation from Egypt "by God's hand." That liberation is, according to an expression of the Kabbalah, "a revelation that comes from On High," or "an awakening of the On High." The Israelites are thus liberated, or they were liberated. This is an initiative that does not belong to them! The Second Pesach is not an imposed ritual, but a demand made by the people. According to the Kabbalah, it is "the awakening of the Below," deriving from the desire of people to be inscribed in the ritual of commemoration and not to be excluded from the community.

There is a big difference between being ordered to be aware of liberty and having the desire for that awareness by oneself. That is perhaps the difference between being liberated and being free. In the course of history, one sees opposition between these two conceptions regarding questions as important as messianism. Must one await the messiah, or must one make him come?

The teaching of the Haggadah here is revolutionary. By citing the text that refers to the Second Pesach, the Haggadah transforms our perspective on the notion of liberty. It is not sufficient to be liberated. One must wish to be free. That is the passage from a being's passivity to its voluntary and desired activity. People are no longer ordered. They are will. They are initiative.

As Martin Buber said: "Tradition is the most beautiful of liberties for the generation that accepts it with clear consciousness of its meaning, but it is also the most miserable slavery for those who receive it as an inheritance through simple spiritual laziness." (Translated from M. Buber, Judaïsme, Verdier, 1985, preface.)

Two quotations from Jean-Paul Sartre sum up perfectly the question of Pesach Sheni and the lesson of korech: "To be free is not at all to be able to do what one wants, but rather to want what one can"; "Liberty is not the liberty to succeed, but the liberty to undertake. To undertake with resolution, a liberty of project, a perpetual project, a creative liberty."

THE JOURNEY OF THE SANCTUARY

The text of the Second Pesach is presented with a different theme. It allows us to understand the meaning of this articulation.

The continuation of the text of the Second Pesach mentions the journey of the Israelites in the desert. The text emphasizes two points. The first is the voyage of the Tabernacle, the place where the divine presence, the Shechina, is in motion, travelling.

Judaism begins with Abraham, with the words that God addressed to Abraham, ordering him to leave: "Lech-lecha"—"Go away from your country, from your homeland, from the house of your *father, to the land that I shall show to you."*

"The demand for uprooting, affirmation of the nomadic truth. That is how he breaks with paganism, all paganism. To be a pagan is to be fixed, to pin a label on oneself, to establish oneself by making a pact with the permanence that authorizes one's presence and certifies the certitude of the soil. Nomadism responds to a relationship that possession does not satisfy. Every time the Jew makes a sign to us in history, it is through the call of a movement." (Translated from Maurice Blanchot, L'entretien infini, *Gallimard, 1969.)*

AN ORDER FROM GOD OR A WORD FROM MOSES?

The second point is the existence of a cloud and of fire that rested upon the Tabernacle, or the "Mishkan," or the sanctuary, as a sign of the presence of God, and the fact that the departures and halts on the journey were dictated by that very cloud.

One of the essential ideas of the biblical text is to underline the importance of human beings in taking responsibility for the dynamism of the divine in the world.

It is not insignificant that Korech, as a reversal of perspective on the question of liberty was formulated by Hillel, one of the first great masters of the Talmud.

The Talmud is a collection of oral interpretations of the biblical text, which means that people have the liberty to interpret the biblical text according to their own sensitivity and subjectivity.

Korech means to bind together, literally, "religion," "a covenant," no longer a covenant founded upon people's passive acceptance of the law, but upon their active and creative engagement.

A passage in the Zohar teaches that "God is text." This means that the most radical manifestation of the divine passes via the text, through the book and the letters of the alphabet, in other words, through an object belonging to this world. It is as though the infinite—God—

passed into the finite and became something finite, too, something limited as every text is limited. This is the cloud and fire of which our text speaks, as confirmed by another text, which speaks of the letters of books as black fire on white fire.

This passage from the infinite to the finite, the possibility of finite to exist on the basis of the infinite has a name in Kabbalah: "tsimtsum," the contraction of God. This contraction presents an important theological question. If God offers Himself to the finite, does He still remain God, an infinite God?

The Kabbalists and Talmudists were well aware of this problem, and they had to respond to it, because, obviously, the risk of having a finite God, a God that has run aground in this world, is to have an idol. And if God makes himself into a book, somehow the text must be given its infinite status. Every means must be used to give it an infinite meaning. That is what the Talmudists managed to do. In the Talmud, it is not a matter of understanding the text better, or of understanding God better. That would be a way of appropriating God, to enclose the infinite. Instead, it is a matter of interpreting the text so that the world that it contains—and which is unique—may be understood in plural fashion.

The definition of the Talmud consists precisely in that plurality of speech due to a plurality of interpretations. One may say one thing about the text, but also something else, and yet another thing: the interpretation never ceases. The Talmud does not state the meaning of the Torah. On the contrary, it constantly opens the Torah to new meanings. That is the meaning of the travels of the Ark and of the camp by the hand of Moses, by human interpretation.

According to Armand Abécassis, "the Jewish people are not the people of the book, but the people of the interpretation of the book." This interpretive vocation is a way of being responsible for God, from God, for the fact that God is alive. God will or will not exist as an infinite being depending on whether people make a static idol or a living being of Him, by passive acceptance of the law or by creative interpretation.

Part Ten

SHULCHAN ORECH

SHULCHAN ORECH

eating the meal

THE LANGUAGE OF FOOD

After the various Seder rituals, we sit down at the table for a festive meal. This is a time both for eating and for taking up the commentaries on the Haggadah again.

The phrase "shulchan orech" rhymes with "korech," and it means to set the table. This expression has had great success in that, in slightly different form, it is the name of one of the greatest codes of Jewish law, the "Shulchan Aruch"—"the Set Table," written by Rabbi Joseph Caro of Safed (1488-1575). The "Shulchan Aruch," printed for the first time in Venice in 1565, is a monumental code that provides access to all of Jewish law, with the exception of the laws regarding the Temple in Jerusalem. Naming a code of Jewish law with an expression concerning the table and food shows the extreme centrality of the laws that organize the act of nourishing.

For Judaism, eating is an ethical and social act. The dietary laws bring out classification mechanisms, operations that identify, distinguish, place in hierarchies, select. In this sense, Jewish food constitutes an act of culture of the first order. Food is a form of language that must be deciphered and learned, the way one learns a foreign language.

Here follows a few rudimentary elements of that foreign language.

CLOVEN HOOF AND CHEWING THE CUD

In Leviticus 11:2-3 we read: "These are the animals that you may eat from among all the land animals: any animal that has true hoofs, with clefts through the hoofs, and that chews the cud—such may you eat."

For meat, there are two imperative criteria to make it edible, or kosher: the animal must have a cloven hoof, and the animal must be a ruminant, thus a vegetarian. The Bible forbids the eating of carnivores because their way of nourishing themselves violates the ideal ethical order.

Defining the category of edible animals with respect to their membership in classes and their relation to the elements, the biblical dietary prescriptions divide the animal world into three classes: animals that walk on land, animals that swim in water, and animals that fly in the air. These categories are presented clearly and above all as a form of organizing the living world. The animals themselves are included in a broader hierarchy: mineral, vegetable, animal, human. This hierarchy must be respected so as to permit the harmony of the world. Thus the animal that one may eat must not have killed an animal in the same or higher category for the purpose of eating it.

The cloven hoof is a sign that the animal does not have claws, and thus that it does not kill in order to nourish itself. This is a distinctive trait, contrasting with the claws with which carnivores are equipped.

The commentators have added a symbolic interpretation, saying that the cloven hoof is a sign of openness, of duality, and of pluralism. If eating is a way of talking and thinking, the openness of the hoof points toward the impossibility of a single word or thought. It is a reminder of the danger of dogmatism and of totalitarianism, even, and above all, in the name of God.

The dimension of rumination is explained as the necessity of thinking and meditating by going over the same ideas several times. The Hebrew word for study is "mishna," which comes from the root "shano," which means "to repeat." To think is not to be content with the ready-made thoughts one finds at the first impulse.

According to the Talmud, Moses did not receive the contents of the Torah on Mount Sinai, but various interpretative keys which, over the centuries, made it possible for an infinite commentary to unfold. Rumination means not accepting an idea or a text as is, but always to take it up again, to interrogate it again, to comment on it, invent, renew, feel the life that palpitates in it and in ourselves.

STUDY AS LIBERTY!

Study is an act of resistance against the "language of institutions." This resistance, a true combat, opens words again to their polysemic possibilities. Everything takes place in the break, in the act of de-signification. Since the unique, unequivocal, monosemic language of the situation is the basis of its totalitarianism, of its intolerance, and of its violence, it is important that, by the act of designification, the human being and his or her words attain or re-attain liberty. A person continually constructs himself by interpretation. His becoming is possible only in the untiring succession of making and unmaking meaning, of reading and unreading of the text. The role of interpretation is clear. It is not a matter of repeating, or paraphrasing the text from which one starts, but literally to take off, to go beyond the verse, to pass from the text to one's own text: passage and Passover.

Leave Egypt. Risk your liberty ...

SHECHITA, OR RITUAL SLAUGHTER:
THE QUESTION OF BLOOD

The animal that satisfies the criteria of having a cloven hoof and chewing its cud must be bled. Ritual slaughter, called "shechita" in Hebrew, has two aims. The first is that the animal should not suffer, and the second is that the animal's *blood must be drained, because blood is completely prohibited, as it is written in Deuteronomy 12: "But make sure that you do not partake of the blood; for the blood is the life, and you must not consume the life with the flesh. You must not partake of it; you must pour it out on the ground like water: you must not partake of it, so that it may go well with you and with your descendants to come, for you will be doing what is right in the eyes of the Lord. But such sacred and votive donations as you may have shall be taken by you to the site that the Lord will choose. You shall offer your burnt offerings, both the flesh and the blood, on the altar of the Lord your God; and of your other sacrifices, the blood shall be poured out on the altar of the Lord your God, and you shall eat the flesh.*

"Be careful to heed all these commandments that I enjoin upon you; thus it will go well with you and with your descendants after you forever, for you will be doing what is good and right in the eyes of the Lord your God."

We now have a better understanding of the prohibition against eating carnivorous animals: just as God forbids humans to nourish themselves from blood, similarly He imposes that law upon animals. The selection of animals by their diets is already an application of that major prohibition in Jewish ethics: that against suppressing life.

BLOOD AND PESACH

The question of blood that we raise here, as though in passing, is in fact central to the Haggadah and Pesach. Everything takes place as though Pesach were a long meditation upon the meaning of blood. The very origin of Pesach cannot be understood without reference to blood. Indeed, if we reread the text of the Haggadah on the meaning of Passover, we will find that the biblical reference text is Exodus 12:13: "And the blood on your houses where you are staying shall be a sign for you: when I see the blood I will pass over you, so that no plague will destroy you when I strike the land of Egypt."

FOODS AND WORDS: COMMENTARY AND SACRIFICE

The word for "blood" in Hebrew also means "silence." One must leave the Egypt of language by accepting the silence of words, by recognizing the breach by which words are emptied of meaning, of their blood, a semantic hemorrhage that opens upon commentary, that offers knowledge to the ear that words exist that one can make into a land to dwell in! There are words that one silences so as to feel within them the expulsion from place, the creative exile.

The foregoing remarks allow us to understand the meaning of the Talmudic text that teaches, "any meal that is eaten without being accompanied by words of Torah is like a sacrifice offered by the dead. Rather, like the consumption of offal." Food must have sacrificial status, which it acquires by words of study pronounced during the meal. Thus, speaking belongs to the order of sacrifice.

By commentary, by the hemorrhage of meaning, words are led to death, to the sacrifice of meaning. The meaning is sacrificed: silence.

It is fundamental to emphasize that for the Talmud, study and prayer, after the destruction of the Temple, replace sacrifice.

SPEECH AND CHILDHOOD

The entire Seder night consists in making way for the speech of the child. Everything is done so that the child won't fall asleep: the game of hide and seek, delicious food, rhymes, songs, theater, etc.

The Seder night is a path toward liberty, and liberty passes through the capacity to bear the dimension of childhood within one.

What is a child?

What is wonderful about children and adolescents is their ability to say, "when I'm big, I'll ..." I will be, I will do.

In that extraordinary little phrase is all the power of dream, of expectation, of impatience, of time to come. In that magic little phrase there is all the power of a marvelous word: hope.

A child is borne by hope. His time is virtually messianic. Rather, the child does not have hope. He is hope itself.

Hope is knowledge that everything is always open, that the future is a gift that life offers us, because one can always transform oneself, change paths, invent new ways without being trapped in the role of "adults," in which we shut ourselves, or in which others have imprisoned us.

"To live is to be born in every moment!"

Now we doubtless understand better the meaning of Rabbi Nachman of Bratslav's saying, "It is forbidden to be old." It is forbidden to lose the power of hope. It is forbidden to give up growing. One must always be able to say, "When I grow up, I'll ..."

But we are touching upon an entirely new definition of old age. A person is old if he has lost hope. A person is old if, instead of seeing hope as a door opening on the future, he sees it as opening on the past.

Old age is the nostalgia of hope. It is when we no longer have enough strength to say, "tomorrow."

Childhood is desire, anguish, crying, and laughing, but above all, the dream, the sacred dream of growing up.

"A great person is someone who does not relinquish his childhood dreams, and an artist is the one who recreates them."

DISTINGUISHING BETWEEN LIFE AND DEATH

Earlier in this commentary, we showed that the slaughter of animals was a form of murder expiated by the sacrificial dimension given to that slaughter and to the status of altar conferred upon the dining table.

Flowing blood thus remains a sign of death, despite all the liturgical acts that try to sublimate that death-bearing dimension. Blood flows from the stricken animal. Milk, however, is biologically the result of a vital process. The prohibition against mixing milk and meat ("basar vechalav") can be viewed as the desire not to mix milk and blood, the product of a vital process with a food resulting from killing.

Thus, in the opposition between meat food and dairy foods, there is the full articulation of the notion of the sanctification of the vital process in the Jewish tradition. Milk is the opposite of all the foods resulting from the flow of blood.

The prescription not to mix dairy foods, the product of a vital process, and meat, resulting from the killing of an animal, only applies to slaughtered animals and fowl, but not to fish, which can be served at a dairy meal, since fish are not sacrificed, and the sign of their death is not the flowing of blood.

Similarly, eggs can be eaten with either dairy or meat meals. But if there is a trace of blood in the yolk, they cannot be eaten at all, because this is the mixture of two contradictory signs, of life and of death.

THE GOD OF ABRAHAM, THE GOD OF ISAAC, THE GOD OF JACOB

While milk is the opposite of blood in Jewish representations and practices, it is also viewed as the food of fecundity and fertility, and it figures in certain festive rituals that one wishes to be beneficial.

That is the case with the Maimuna, a popular festival that closes the Passover holiday and marks the ends of its restrictions. This is also the case with the holiday of Shavuoth, which commemorates the giving of the Torah, where at least the first meal of the holiday is a dairy meal.

This last remark would appear to lead us to another interpretation of the prohibition against mixing milk and meat. The custom of drinking milk on Shavuoth comes from the fact that the Torah is regarded as a food that permits one to grow and mature.

"You shall not cook a kid in its mother's milk," can be understood to mean "you will not raise the child, you will not have him mature, with the same values as its mother."

This is an ethical and pedagogical imperative. Every generation needs a language that will be its own.

The Jewish liturgy contains an interesting text that says, "God of Abraham, God of Isaac, and God of Jacob..." Why do we not say, "God of Abraham, Isaac, and Jacob"? Why repeat the word "God" three times? After all, it's the same God!

This is because the perception of God by Abraham is not the same as that of Isaac or of Jacob, and vice versa. Every generation must have its own comprehension and interpretation of the world.

Even if we are dealing with the same God, with the same values, the subjective perception that everyone has of it is totally different. This plural God gives us a living God, not polytheism, but a plural Judaism, liberty for everyone to perceive his own relationship with the divine.

History is not repetition but invention and novelty.

This also brings to mind a Hasidic story:

One day a Rabbi assembled all of his disciples and invited them to ask questions and even to express criticism. The disciples said to him:

"Master, your behavior astonishes us. You never do what your father, your master, did, whom we knew before he chose you as his successor. How do you regard yourself as his heritage? Where is your fidelity?"

The Rabbi gave his disciples a serious look, but in the depths of his eyes there shone a spark of joy and wit. He said to them:

"I shall explain to you. There is no one more faithful than I! I do exactly, in every respect, what my father did. Just as he never imitated anyone, neither do I!"

Part Eleven

TZAFUN

צָפוּן

TZAFUN

finishing the meal with the afikoman

ONE TAKES THE MATZAH THAT WAS SET ASIDE FOR THE AFIKOMAN AND EATS IT
WHILE RECLINING TO THE LEFT SIDE. IT IS PREFERABLE TO EAT THE AFIKOMAN
BEFORE MIDNIGHT. IT IS FORBIDDEN TO EAT ANYTHING AFTER THE AFIKOMAN
SO THAT THE TASTE OF MATZAH REMAINS IN ONE'S MOUTH.

After the meal, one takes a piece of the matzah that had been hidden at the beginning of
the meal and looked for by the children or the parents, as we explained in the section entitled
"Yachatz." That matzah has two names: "tzafun," which means "hidden," according to the tradition
we have just mentioned, and it is also called the "afikoman."

The eleventh part of the Seder consists in eating that afikoman. It is eaten in memory of the
paschal sacrifice, the Pesach, or, according to other commentators, in memory of the matzah itself.
The idea is to finish the evening with the taste that constitutes its essence. The piece of afikoman
replaces dessert, or completes the dessert. In fact, the word afikoman derives from the Greek, and it
signifies the end of a meal that was characterized by singing and dancing to the music of a flute,
by nightly visits to the homes of all the guests in order to eat some more, to drink, and amuse
oneself. According to the text of the Mishnah, that is the answer that one gives to the question of
the wise son: one does not conclude the Passover meal with an Afikoman. In other words, the Pesach
meal does not end with that sort of nocturnal visit. Thus the word "afikoman" must be understood
as "that which replaces the afikoman."

Certain Hasidic masters like Rabbi Nachman of Bratslav and his disciple Rabbi Nathan treat
the word "afikoman" as Aramaic, "afiko-man," meaning: "make the manna come out."

This is one of the most important teachings of the Pesach holiday, and here is the commentary.

THE BREAD OF QUESTIONS

Let us recall that the manna fell from the sky to the surface of the desert for forty years. Manna
is the bread from the sky whose first appearance is described in Exodus 16:4: "And the Lord said to
Moses, 'I will rain down bread for you from the sky, and the people shall go out and gather each day
that day's portion—that I may thus test them, to see whether they will follow My instructions or not.'"

Later on, in verses 13-15 we read: "In the morning there was a fall of dew about the camp. When the fall of dew lifted, there, over the surface of the wilderness, lay a fine and flaky substance, as fine as frost on the ground. When the Israelites saw it, they said to one another, 'What is it?'– for they did not know what it was."

Then in verse 31: "The house of Israel named it manna; it was like coriander seed, white, and it tasted like wafers in honey."

This manna, the bread from the sky, is a reality that leaps out into the world: an absolute novelty, an event, a break in the fabric of the world.

Before this novelty, "chidush" in Hebrew (used particularly for a new interpretation), the people in the desert, undergoing the experience of liberation from Egypt, stifled their voices. No word comes to them to name this strange apparition.

Everyone said to his neighbor, "What is it?" and they called it, "What is it?" or "manna."

Thus, during the entire journey through the desert, for forty years, the Israelites ate "what is it?" This was a founding experience in that space between two lands, where the apprenticeship of liberty and of the word was formed.

To be free is constantly to keep a distance from the world, not to be grabbed up immediately in the "spider web" of ideologically prefabricated meaning. To be free is to retain an attitude of questioning before the world and to be capable of seeing in it, every time, the dawn that begins again. The biblical text on the manna is rich in detail and of foremost importance.

Again in chapter 16, verse 32, we find: "Moses said, 'This is what the Lord has commanded: Let one omer of it be kept throughout the ages, in order that they may see the bread that I fed you in the wilderness when I brought you out from the land of Egypt.'

"And Moses said to Aaron, 'Take a jar, put one omer of manna in it, and place it before the

Lord, to be kept throughout the ages.'"

Thus a measure of manna was kept for succeeding generations. Thus the memory of the manna is one of the ten memories mentioned every day in morning prayers.

Every generation must retain the force of questioning the world in a new way.

Regarding the manna, the Bible also says (Exodus 16:19-21): "And Moses said to them, 'Let no one leave any of it over until morning.' But they paid no attention to Moses; some of them left of it until morning, and it became infested with maggots and stank. And Moses was angry with them. So they gathered it every morning, each as much as he needed to eat; for when the sun grew hot, it would melt."

This passage adds an important element to our reflection on manna as a question: the manna could not be conserved. Astonishment before the world cannot be acquired once and for all. Each time, one must begin the difficult job of withdrawing not only with respect to knowledge but also with respect to the question. A question that has become habitual is no longer questioning.

However, a question can and must be asked, day after day, indefatigably, but without its becoming simply a catalogue or museum of questions asked and answers given, deposited as though by obligation.

The "not letting the manna rot until the morning" establishes a philosophy of questioning that transforms the world.

Through questioning, the world that "is" loses all affirmation of being; all of its certitude of being becomes pure possibility: the wisdom of uncertainty.

Hence the Jewish joke that a Jew always responds to a question with another question is not simply a witticism.

Humanity is a "what is it?" In a fine expression, Jabès writes:

"The Jew does not just ask questions: he himself has become a question."

Jabès also writes: "To be is to interrogate in the labyrinth of the question asked of someone else and of God and which has no answer." (Translated from Le Livre des questions, *Gallimard, 1997.)*

The "not letting the manna rot until the morning" is taking up the questioning indefatigably.

THE QUESTION AND TIME

Let us underscore the following extraordinary fact: in Hebrew, the expression, "here is the manna," is "ze man." These two words can also be read and pronounced as "zman," which means "time."

The word "time" in Hebrew originates in "here is the manna." Here is the questioning that remains questioning. In other words, it is the capacity of questioning which, by the possible renewing of meaning, produces time!

In addition, the Hebrew verb "lehazmin," based on the root "zman," means both "to invite someone" and "to make time." The ethic of the Haggadah and of Pesach, which begins and ends by opening a door for another person, is an eminent way of constructing time by that capacity to keep questions open, too. That is to say, not to confine the world, nor oneself, nor others in a definitive definition. To invite someone is to permit him to discover the questions that open the secrets of time for him—of his memory and of his future at the same time.

Part Twelve

BARECH

BARECH

reciting the grace after the meal

FILL THE THIRD CUP WITH WINE
AND RECITE THE BIRKHAT HAMAZON.

שִׁיר הַמַּעֲלוֹת. בְּשׁוּב יְיָ אֶת־שִׁיבַת צִיּוֹן, הָיִינוּ כְּחֹלְמִים:
אָז יִמָּלֵא שְׂחוֹק פִּינוּ, וּלְשׁוֹנֵנוּ רִנָּה. אָז יֹאמְרוּ בַגּוֹיִם,
הִגְדִּיל יְיָ לַעֲשׂוֹת עִם־אֵלֶּה: הִגְדִּיל יְיָ לַעֲשׂוֹת עִמָּנוּ, הָיִינוּ
שְׂמֵחִים: שׁוּבָה יְיָ אֶת־שְׁבִיתֵנוּ, כַּאֲפִיקִים בַּנֶּגֶב: הַזֹּרְעִים
בְּדִמְעָה, בְּרִנָּה יִקְצֹרוּ: הָלוֹךְ יֵלֵךְ וּבָכֹה, נֹשֵׂא מֶשֶׁךְ־הַזָּרַע,
בֹּא־יָבֹא בְרִנָּה נֹשֵׂא אֲלֻמֹּתָיו:

A song of Ascents. When God returns the captives of Zion,
we will be like dreamers. Then our mouth will be filled with laughter
and our tongue with song. Then they will say among the nations:
"Great things has God done for them!" Great things God has done for us,
for which we are very happy! Bring back, God, our prisoners,
like flowing streams in dry land. They that sow in tears,
shall harvest with rejoicing. He who cried while carrying the seed,
will return with joy, bearing his bundles of sheaves.

רַבּוֹתַי נְבָרֵךְ:

יְהִי שֵׁם יְיָ מְבֹרָךְ, מֵעַתָּה וְעַד עוֹלָם:

יְהִי שֵׁם יְיָ מְבֹרָךְ, מֵעַתָּה וְעַד עוֹלָם:
בִּרְשׁוּת מָרָנָן וְרַבָּנָן וְרַבּוֹתַי,
נְבָרֵךְ (אֱלֹהֵינוּ) שֶׁאָכַלְנוּ מִשֶּׁלּוֹ.

בָּרוּךְ (אֱלֹהֵינוּ) שֶׁאָכַלְנוּ מִשֶּׁלּוֹ וּבְטוּבוֹ חָיִינוּ:

THE HANDS ARE THEN WASHED. WHEN THERE
ARE AT LEAST THREE MALES, THIRTEEN YEARS
OR OLDER, BEGIN HERE (FOR TEN OR MORE
MALES ADD THE WORDS, "OUR GOD").

HOST:

Gentlemen,
we want to say Grace!

GUESTS:

Blessed is the Name of God,
from this time and forever.

HOST:

Blessed is the Name of God,
from this time and forever.
With your permission,
let us bless (our God),
Whose food we have eaten!

GUESTS:

Blessed be (our God) Whose
food we have eaten and through
Whose goodness we live.

THE WINE AND THE SECRET (JEREMIAH 25:15)

בָּרוּךְ (אֱלֹהֵינוּ) שֶׁאָכַלְנוּ מִשֶּׁלוֹ וּבְטוּבוֹ חָיִינוּ:

בָּרוּךְ הוּא וּבָרוּךְ שְׁמוֹ:

בָּרוּךְ אַתָּה יְיָ, אֱלֹהֵינוּ, מֶלֶךְ הָעוֹלָם, הַזָּן אֶת־הָעוֹלָם כֻּלּוֹ,
בְּטוּבוֹ בְּחֵן בְּחֶסֶד וּבְרַחֲמִים, הוּא נוֹתֵן לֶחֶם לְכָל־בָּשָׂר,
כִּי לְעוֹלָם חַסְדּוֹ: וּבְטוּבוֹ הַגָּדוֹל תָּמִיד לֹא־חָסַר לָנוּ, וְאַל
יֶחְסַר־לָנוּ מָזוֹן לְעוֹלָם וָעֶד, בַּעֲבוּר שְׁמוֹ הַגָּדוֹל:

HOST:

Blessed be (our God) Whose
food we have eaten and through
Whose goodness we live.

ALL:

Blessed is He!

IF THREE ADULT MALES ARE NOT PRESENT,
THEN BEGIN HERE:

Blessed are You, God,
King of the universe,
Who feeds the whole world
with His goodness, with grace,
loving kindness and mercy.
He gives food to all flesh,
for His love is endless.
In His great goodness,
we have never lacked, and never
will lack sustenance, forever,
for the sake of His great Name;

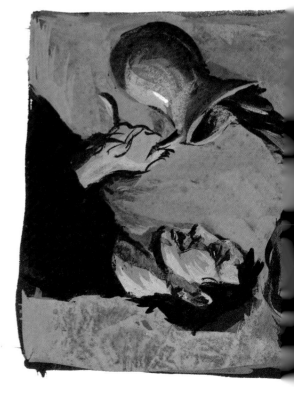

for He is God Who feeds and sustains all, Who does good to all, and prepares food for all His creatures which He created. As it is written: "Your hand is open, satisfying the desire of all life." Blessed are You, God, Who compassionately gives food to all.

We thank You, God, that You gave our fathers a desirable, good and ample land; that You brought us out from Egypt and delivered us from slavery; that You sealed Your covenant in our flesh; that You taught us You Torah; and that You made Your laws known to us; and for the life, grace and loving kindness with which You have favored us, and for the food which You constantly provide and sustain us, every day, at all times and at every hour.

For all this, God, we give thanks to You and bless You; praised be Your Name in the mouths of all life, always and forever. As it is written:

כִּי הוּא אֵל זָן וּמְפַרְנֵס לַכֹּל, וּמֵטִיב לַכֹּל, וּמֵכִין מָזוֹן לְכָל־בְּרִיּוֹתָיו, אֲשֶׁר בָּרָא. בָּרוּךְ אַתָּה יְיָ, הַזָּן אֶת הַכֹּל:

נוֹדֶה לְּךָ, יְיָ אֱלֹהֵינוּ, עַל שֶׁהִנְחַלְתָּ לַאֲבוֹתֵינוּ אֶרֶץ חֶמְדָּה טוֹבָה וּרְחָבָה, וְעַל שֶׁהוֹצֵאתָנוּ, יְיָ אֱלֹהֵינוּ, מֵאֶרֶץ מִצְרַיִם, וּפְדִיתָנוּ מִבֵּית עֲבָדִים, וְעַל בְּרִיתְךָ שֶׁחָתַמְתָּ בִּבְשָׂרֵנוּ, וְעַל תּוֹרָתְךָ שֶׁלִּמַּדְתָּנוּ, וְעַל חֻקֶּיךָ שֶׁהוֹדַעְתָּנוּ, וְעַל חַיִּים, חֵן וָחֶסֶד שֶׁחוֹנַנְתָּנוּ, וְעַל אֲכִילַת מָזוֹן, שָׁאַתָּה זָן וּמְפַרְנֵס אוֹתָנוּ תָּמִיד, בְּכָל־יוֹם וּבְכָל־עֵת וּבְכָל־שָׁעָה:

וְעַל הַכֹּל, יְיָ אֱלֹהֵינוּ, אֲנַחְנוּ מוֹדִים לָךְ, וּמְבָרְכִים אוֹתָךְ, יִתְבָּרַךְ שִׁמְךָ בְּפִי כָּל־חַי תָּמִיד, לְעוֹלָם וָעֶד: כַּכָּתוּב.

"You should eat, be satiated
and you shall bless God for the
good land that He gave you"
(Deuteronomy 8:10).
**Blessed are you, God,
for the Land and for the food.**

וְאָכַלְתָּ וְשָׂבָעְתָּ, וּבֵרַכְתָּ אֶת יְיָ
אֱלֹהֶיךָ, עַל־הָאָרֶץ הַטֹּבָה אֲשֶׁר
נָתַן לָךְ. בָּרוּךְ אַתָּה יְיָ, עַל־
הָאָרֶץ וְעַל־הַמָּזוֹן:

Have mercy, God,
on Your people Israel;
on Your city Jerusalem;
on Zion home of Your glory;
on the royal house of David,
Your chosen; and on the great
and Holy Temple which
is called by Your Name.

רַחֵם, יְיָ אֱלֹהֵינוּ, עַל יִשְׂרָאֵל
עַמֶּךָ, וְעַל יְרוּשָׁלַיִם עִירֶךָ, וְעַל
צִיּוֹן מִשְׁכַּן כְּבוֹדֶךָ, וְעַל מַלְכוּת
בֵּית דָּוִד מְשִׁיחֶךָ, וְעַל־הַבַּיִת
הַגָּדוֹל וְהַקָּדוֹשׁ שֶׁנִּקְרָא שִׁמְךָ
עָלָיו:

Our God, our Father, tend us,
feed us, nourish and sustains us.
Grant us relief quickly,
God, from all our troubles.
Let us, God, never be dependent
upon the gifts of men,
nor upon their loans,
but we should depend
only on Your full open Hand
that is holy and generous,
so that we may neither be
shamed nor disgraced for ever.

אֱלֹהֵינוּ, אָבִינוּ, רְעֵנוּ, זוּנֵנוּ,
פַּרְנְסֵנוּ, וְכַלְכְּלֵנוּ, וְהַרְוִיחֵנוּ,
וְהַרְוַח לָנוּ יְיָ אֱלֹהֵינוּ מְהֵרָה
מִכָּל צָרוֹתֵינוּ, וְנָא, אַל
תַּצְרִיכֵנוּ יְיָ אֱלֹהֵינוּ, לֹא לִידֵי
מַתְּנַת בָּשָׂר וָדָם, וְלֹא לִידֵי
הַלְוָאָתָם. כִּי אִם לְיָדְךָ הַמְּלֵאָה,
הַפְּתוּחָה, הַקְּדוֹשָׁה וְהָרְחָבָה,
שֶׁלֹּא נֵבוֹשׁ וְלֹא נִכָּלֵם לְעוֹלָם
וָעֶד:

(ON SHABBAT, ADD:

Be pleased, God,
and strengthen us,
through Your commandments
and through the commandment
of the Seventh day, this great
and holy Shabbat. For this day
is great and holy before You,
that we may rest and relax
in it from all work, in love,
as You desire. May it be Your will,
God, to grant us that we have
no trouble, sorrow or grief
on our day of rest.
Let us, God, merit to see
the consolation of Zion, Your city,
and the rebuilding of Jerusalem,
Your city of holiness,
for You are the Master
of salvation and comfort.)

רְצֵה וְהַחֲלִיצֵנוּ, יְיָ אֱלֹהֵינוּ,
בְּמִצְוֹתֶיךָ, וּבְמִצְוַת יוֹם
הַשְּׁבִיעִי, הַשַּׁבָּת הַגָּדוֹל
וְהַקָּדוֹשׁ הַזֶּה, כִּי יוֹם זֶה גָּדוֹל
וְקָדוֹשׁ הוּא לְפָנֶיךָ, לִשְׁבָּת־בּוֹ
וְלָנוּחַ בּוֹ בְּאַהֲבָה כְּמִצְוַת
רְצוֹנֶךָ. בִּרְצוֹנְךָ הָנִיחַ לָנוּ, יְיָ
אֱלֹהֵינוּ, שֶׁלֹּא תְהֵא צָרָה וְיָגוֹן
וַאֲנָחָה בְּיוֹם מְנוּחָתֵנוּ, וְהַרְאֵנוּ,
יְיָ אֱלֹהֵינוּ, בְּנֶחָמַת צִיּוֹן עִירֶךָ,
וּבְבִנְיַן יְרוּשָׁלַיִם עִיר קָדְשֶׁךָ, כִּי
אַתָּה הוּא בַּעַל הַיְשׁוּעוֹת וּבַעַל
הַנֶּחָמוֹת:

God, God of our fathers,
may there rise, come, reach, be
seen, find favor, be understood,
be recalled and remembered
before You—our remembrance,
and the remembrance
of our fathers; the remembrance
of Mashiach, the son of David,
Your servant; the remembrance
of Jerusalem, Your holy city,
and the remembrance of Your
people, Israel, for deliverance,
for good, for grace, for loving
kindness and for mercy,
for good life and for peace,
on this Festival of matzot.
Remember us on it, God,
for goodness, recall us on it
for blessing, and save us on it
for good life. With the promise
of salvation and mercy, favor
and be gracious to us,
have mercy upon us and help us.
For to You alone our eyes
are turned, for You, God, are
a gracious and merciful King.

אֱלֹהֵינוּ וֵאלֹהֵי אֲבוֹתֵינוּ.
יַעֲלֶה וְיָבֹא וְיַגִּיעַ וְיֵרָאֶה וְיֵרָצֶה
וְיִשָּׁמַע וְיִפָּקֵד וְיִזָּכֵר זִכְרוֹנֵנוּ
וּפִקְדוֹנֵנוּ, וְזִכְרוֹן אֲבוֹתֵינוּ.
וְזִכְרוֹן מָשִׁיחַ בֶּן־דָּוִד עַבְדֶּךָ.
וְזִכְרוֹן יְרוּשָׁלַיִם עִיר קָדְשֶׁךָ.
וְזִכְרוֹן כָּל־עַמְּךָ בֵּית יִשְׂרָאֵל
לְפָנֶיךָ. לִפְלֵיטָה לְטוֹבָה וּלְחֵן
וּלְחֶסֶד וּלְרַחֲמִים לְחַיִּים
וּלְשָׁלוֹם בְּיוֹם חַג הַמַּצּוֹת הַזֶּה.
זָכְרֵנוּ יְיָ אֱלֹהֵינוּ בּוֹ לְטוֹבָה.
וּפָקְדֵנוּ בוֹ לִבְרָכָה. וְהוֹשִׁיעֵנוּ
בוֹ לְחַיִּים. וּבִדְבַר יְשׁוּעָה
וְרַחֲמִים חוּס וְחָנֵּנוּ, וְרַחֵם
עָלֵינוּ וְהוֹשִׁיעֵנוּ, כִּי אֵלֶיךָ
עֵינֵינוּ, כִּי אֵל מֶלֶךְ חַנּוּן וְרַחוּם
אָתָּה:

וּבְנֵה יְרוּשָׁלַיִם, עִיר הַקֹּדֶשׁ, בִּמְהֵרָה בְיָמֵינוּ. בָּרוּךְ אַתָּה יְיָ, בּוֹנֵה בְרַחֲמָיו יְרוּשָׁלָיִם. אָמֵן:

בָּרוּךְ אַתָּה יְיָ, אֱלֹהֵינוּ, מֶלֶךְ הָעוֹלָם, הָאֵל אָבִינוּ, מַלְכֵּנוּ, אַדִּירֵנוּ, בּוֹרְאֵנוּ, גּוֹאֲלֵנוּ, יוֹצְרֵנוּ, קְדוֹשֵׁנוּ, קְדוֹשׁ יַעֲקֹב, רוֹעֵנוּ, רוֹעֵה יִשְׂרָאֵל, הַמֶּלֶךְ הַטּוֹב וְהַמֵּטִיב לַכֹּל. שֶׁבְּכָל־יוֹם וָיוֹם הוּא הֵטִיב, הוּא מֵטִיב, הוּא יֵיטִיב לָנוּ.

Rebuild Jerusalem, the Holy
City, soon in our days. Blessed
are You, God, Who rebuilds
Jerusalem in His mercy. Amen.

Blessed are You, God,
King of the universe, Almighty,
our father, our King, our Ruler,
our Creator, our Redeemer,
our Maker, our Holy One,
the Holy One of Yaakov,
our Shepherd, the Shepherd
of Israel, the good King,
the benevolent King—
Who each and every day,
did good, does good and
will do good to us.

הוּא גְמָלָנוּ, הוּא גוֹמְלֵנוּ, הוּא יִגְמְלֵנוּ לָעַד לְחֵן וּלְחֶסֶד
וּלְרַחֲמִים וּלְרֶוַח, הַצָּלָה וְהַצְלָחָה, בְּרָכָה וִישׁוּעָה, נֶחָמָה,
פַּרְנָסָה וְכַלְכָּלָה וְרַחֲמִים וְחַיִּים וְשָׁלוֹם וְכָל־טוֹב, וּמִכָּל־
טוּב לְעוֹלָם אַל־יְחַסְּרֵנוּ:

הָרַחֲמָן. הוּא יִמְלוֹךְ עָלֵינוּ לְעוֹלָם וָעֶד:
הָרַחֲמָן. הוּא יִתְבָּרַךְ בַּשָּׁמַיִם וּבָאָרֶץ:
הָרַחֲמָן. הוּא יִשְׁתַּבַּח לְדוֹר דּוֹרִים וְיִתְפָּאַר בָּנוּ לְנֵצַח
נְצָחִים וְיִתְהַדַּר בָּנוּ לָעַד וּלְעוֹלְמֵי עוֹלָמִים:

It is He who has granted us,
does grant us, and will
forever grant us with grace,
loving kindness, mercy, relief,
salvation, success, blessing, help,
comfort, food and sustenance,
mercy, life, peace and all good;
and with all manner of good
things—may He never deprive us.

May the Merciful reign
over us forever and ever!
May the Merciful be praised
in heaven and on earth!
May the Merciful be praised
for all generations, may He be
glorified through us forever
and ever, and may He be
honored through us for all
eternity! May the Merciful grant
us our needs with honor!

May be the Merciful
break the yoke from our necks
and lead us upright to our land!
May the Merciful
send abundant blessing
to this house and upon this table
from which we have eaten!
May the Merciful
send us the prophet Eliyahu,
of blessed memory,
and that he bring
to us good tidings,
salvations and consolations!
May the Merciful, bless:

הָרַחֲמָן. הוּא יְפַרְנְסֵנוּ בְּכָבוֹד:
הָרַחֲמָן. הוּא יִשְׁבּוֹר עֻלֵּנוּ מֵעַל
צַוָּארֵנוּ וְהוּא יוֹלִיכֵנוּ קוֹמְמִיּוּת
לְאַרְצֵנוּ: הָרַחֲמָן. הוּא יִשְׁלַח
בְּרָכָה מְרֻבָּה בַּבַּיִת הַזֶּה וְעַל
שֻׁלְחָן זֶה שֶׁאָכַלְנוּ עָלָיו:
הָרַחֲמָן. הוּא יִשְׁלַח לָנוּ אֶת־
אֵלִיָּהוּ הַנָּבִיא, זָכוּר לַטּוֹב,
וִיבַשֶּׂר־לָנוּ בְּשׂוֹרוֹת טוֹבוֹת
יְשׁוּעוֹת וְנֶחָמוֹת: הָרַחֲמָן. הוּא
יְבָרֵךְ

THE CHILDREN AT THE TABLE
OF THEIR FATHER SAY:

My father, master
of this house, and
my mother, mistress
of this house, all that
sit here, them and
their house and
family, together with
all that is theirs;

אֶת־אָבִי מוֹרִי, בַּעַל הַבַּיִת הַזֶּה,
וְאֶת־אִמִּי מוֹרָתִי, בַּעֲלַת הַבַּיִת
הַזֶּה, אוֹתָם וְאֶת־בֵּיתָם וְאֶת־
זַרְעָם, וְאֶת כָּל־אֲשֶׁר לָהֶם,

THE HEAD OF THE FAMILY:

Me, my wife
and family and
all that is mine;

אוֹתִי וְאֶת־אִשְׁתִּי וְאֶת־בֵּיתִי
(וְאֶת־זַרְעִי) וְאֶת כָּל־אֲשֶׁר לִי,

THE WIFE, AT HOME:

Me, my husband
and family and
all that is mine;

אוֹתִי וְאֶת־בַּעְלִי (וְאֶת־זַרְעִי)
וְאֶת כָּל־אֲשֶׁר לִי,

A GUEST SAYS:

The head of this house;
he, his wife, his children
and all that is him.
(In the presence of a large
audience, add: and all the people
who are around this table.)

Us, and all that is ours,
just as our fathers Avraham,
Yitzchak and Yaakov
were blessed in all,
through all, and with all.
May He bless us, all,
with a complete blessing!
To that we say: Amen!

(וֹ)אֶת־רַב בַּעַל הַבַּיִת הַזֶּה,
אוֹתוֹ וְאֶת־אִשְׁתּוֹ וְאֶת־בֵּיתוֹ
וְאֶת־זַרְעוֹ, וְאֶת כָּל־אֲשֶׁר לוֹ,

(וֹ)אֶת־כָּל־הַמְסֻבִּין כָּאן,

אוֹתָנוּ וְאֶת כָּל־אֲשֶׁר לָנוּ, כְּמוֹ
שֶׁנִּתְבָּרְכוּ אֲבוֹתֵינוּ אַבְרָהָם,
יִצְחָק וְיַעֲקֹב בַּכֹּל, מִכֹּל, כֹּל, כֵּן
יְבָרֵךְ אוֹתָנוּ כֻּלָנוּ יַחַד בִּבְרָכָה
שְׁלֵמָה. וְנֹאמַר אָמֵן:

On High, may merit
be accepted about them
and about us,
so as to assure peace.
May we receive
as blessing from God
and charity from the God
Who saves us;
and let us find favor
and understanding
in the eyes of God and man.

בַּמָּרוֹם יְלַמְּדוּ עֲלֵיהֶם וְעָלֵינוּ
זְכוּת שֶׁתְּהֵא לְמִשְׁמֶרֶת שָׁלוֹם.
וְנִשָּׂא בְרָכָה מֵאֵת יְיָ וּצְדָקָה
מֵאֱלֹהֵי יִשְׁעֵנוּ. וְנִמְצָא חֵן
וְשֵׂכֶל טוֹב בְּעֵינֵי אֱלֹהִים וְאָדָם:

(ON SHABBAT:

May the Merciful
bequeath to us the day
that will be all Shabbat
and rest in eternal life!)

הָרַחֲמָן, הוּא יַנְחִילֵנוּ יוֹם שֶׁכֻּלּוֹ
שַׁבָּת וּמְנוּחָה לְחַיֵּי הָעוֹלָמִים:

May the Merciful bequeath to us
the day which is all good.

הָרַחֲמָן, הוּא יַנְחִילֵנוּ יוֹם שֶׁכֻּלּוֹ
טוֹב:

May the Merciful make us
worthy to merit reaching
the days of Mashiach and
to the life of the world to Come!

הָרַחֲמָן. הוּא יְזַכֵּנוּ לִימוֹת
הַמָּשִׁיחַ וּלְחַיֵּי הָעוֹלָם הַבָּא:

He is the tower of salvation to his (chosen) king, and does kindness to His anointed, David, and to his seed forever. He Who makes peace in His place on High; may He also bring peace upon all of us and for all Israel, and say: Amen!

מִגְדוֹל יְשׁוּעוֹת מַלְכּוֹ וְעֹשֶׂה חֶסֶד לִמְשִׁיחוֹ לְדָוִד וּלְזַרְעוֹ עַד עוֹלָם: עֹשֶׂה שָׁלוֹם בִּמְרוֹמָיו הוּא יַעֲשֶׂה שָׁלוֹם עָלֵינוּ וְעַל כָּל יִשְׂרָאֵל. וְאִמְרוּ אָמֵן:

Fear God, His Holy ones, for they will not lack anything—those who fear Him. Young lions suffer and are hungry, but they that seek God will not be in want of any good." (Psalms 34:10,11). Give thanks to God, for He is good, His loving kindness endures forever. (Psalms 118:1). Open Your hand and satisfy the need of all that lives (Psalms 145:16). Blessed is the man that puts his trust in God, and to whom God becomes his trust (Jeremiah 17:7).

יְראוּ אֶת־יְיָ קְדֹשָׁיו, כִּי אֵין מַחְסוֹר לִירֵאָיו: כְּפִירִים רָשׁוּ וְרָעֵבוּ, וְדוֹרְשֵׁי יְיָ לֹא־יַחְסְרוּ כָל־טוֹב: הוֹדוּ לַייָ כִּי טוֹב, כִּי לְעוֹלָם חַסְדּוֹ: פּוֹתֵחַ אֶת יָדֶךְ וּמַשְׂבִּיעַ לְכָל־חַי רָצוֹן: בָּרוּךְ הַגֶּבֶר אֲשֶׁר יִבְטַח בַּייָ וְהָיָה יְיָ מִבְטַחוֹ:

I was young and have now grown old, yet I have never seen a righteous man abandoned, nor his children begging for bread (Psalms 37:25). God will give strength to His people, God will bless His people with peace (Psalms 29:10).

נַעַר הָיִיתִי גַם זָקַנְתִּי וְלֹא רָאִיתִי צַדִּיק נֶעֱזָב וְזַרְעוֹ מְבַקֶּשׁ לָחֶם: יְיָ עֹז לְעַמּוֹ יִתֵּן יְיָ יְבָרֵךְ אֶת עַמּוֹ בַשָּׁלוֹם:

בָּרוּךְ אַתָּה יְיָ אֱלֹהֵינוּ מֶלֶךְ הָעוֹלָם
בּוֹרֵא פְּרִי הַגָּפֶן:

Blessed are You, God, King of the universe,
Who created the fruit of the vine.

THE CUP IS THEN DRUNK WHILE LEANING TO THE LEFT SIDE.

THE FOURTH CUP IS POURED. ONE ALSO POURS A SPECIAL CUP OF WINE, CALLED THE CUP OF ÉLIYAHU (THE PROPHET
ELIJAH; SOME PLACE THIS CUP ON THE TABLE AT THE BEGINNING OF THE SEDER). THE FRONT DOOR IS THEN OPENED
TO SHOW THAT THIS IS THE "NIGHT OF PROTECTION" AND THERE IS NO NEED TO FEAR ANYONE OR ANYTHING.

שְׁפֹךְ חֲמָתְךָ אֶל־הַגּוֹיִם אֲשֶׁר לֹא־יְדָעוּךָ וְעַל־מַמְלָכוֹת
אֲשֶׁר בְּשִׁמְךָ לֹא קָרָאוּ: כִּי־אָכַל אֶת־יַעֲקֹב וְאֶת־נָוֵהוּ
הֵשַׁמּוּ: שְׁפָךְ־עֲלֵיהֶם זַעְמֶךָ וַחֲרוֹן אַפְּךָ יַשִּׂיגֵם: תִּרְדֹּף בְּאַף
וְתַשְׁמִידֵם מִתַּחַת שְׁמֵי יְיָ:

(God) Pour out Your anger upon the nations that do not recognize You,
and upon the Kingdoms that do not call Your Name.
For they have devoured Yaakov and destroyed his dwelling.
Pour Your wrath upon them and let Your burning fury overtake them.
Pursue them with anger and destroy them from beneath the heavens of God.

THE DOOR IS CLOSED.

BARECH

reciting the grace after the meal

After the meal, one recites Birkat Hamazon, the collection of benedictions thanking God
for providing the nourishment necessary for our subsistence. These benedictions are preceded
by Psalm 126, which speaks of the return of the exiles to Jerusalem, a psalm of hope and gratitude
for God's loyalty to his people.

After Psalm 126, someone pronounces the Zimun, the invitation. In general, this is the occasion
for the guests to honor and thank the master and mistress of the house for their invitation.

Beyond this gratitude of humanity to God, Birkat Hamazon also reminds us at the end of every
meal of the fundamental importance of gratitude for the good things one has received.

The feeling of gratitude is central to the Jewish ethic, as shown in the example of King David.
When he fled from his son Avshalom, he was taken in by Barzilai the Gileadite. (2 Samuel 17).

Years later, when David feels his end his near, he calls his son Solomon to tell him his final
will, his ultimate message, if one may say so. (1 Kings 2).

David speaks to Solomon: "I am going the way of all the earth; be strong and show yourself
a man. Keep charge of the Lord your God, walking in his ways and following His laws, His
commandments, His rules, and His admonitions as recorded in the Teaching of Moses, in order
that you may succeed in whatever you undertake and wherever you turn. Then the Lord will
fulfill the promise He made concerning me: 'If your descendants are scrupulous in their conduct,
and walk before Me faithfully, with all their heart and soul, your line on the throne of Israel
shall never end!'"

Regarding his enemies, David adds: "Moreover, you know, too, what Joab the son of Zeruiah
did to me, and what he did to the two captains of the hosts of Israel, to Abner the son of Ner, and
to Amasa, the son of Jether, whom he slew, and shed the blood of war in peace, and put the blood
of war on his girdle that was about his loins and in his shoes that were on his feet. Do therefore
according to your wisdom and let not his gray head go down to the underworld in peace. But show
kindness to the sons of Barzilai the Gileadite and let them be of those who eat at your table; for so
they came to me when I fled because of Avshalom your brother."

Thus he gives an important instruction: show loyalty to the descendents of Barzilai the
Gileadite, and greet them at your table, because they saved David, when he was pursued by
Avshalom. The good they did for him will be returned forever.

The Midrash adds that when the Queen of Sheba came to visit King Solomon, the son of David, she was invited to a great banquet given in her honor. Solomon presented all of the dignitaries to the queen. When she came to Barzilai, she asked of what he was the minister. They answered her, of nothing.

The queen was astonished. Then Solomon told her about his father's will. The Queen of Sheba was so impressed by this behavior of giving good for good, gratitude from generation to generation, that she wanted to belong to that people. That is how, regardless of any political consideration, the Queen of Sheba came to marry Solomon. As for this anecdote, the following point, hardly trivial, can be made: the Falashas of Ethiopia are regarded as descendants of the Queen of Sheba and her union with Solomon.

Part Thirteen

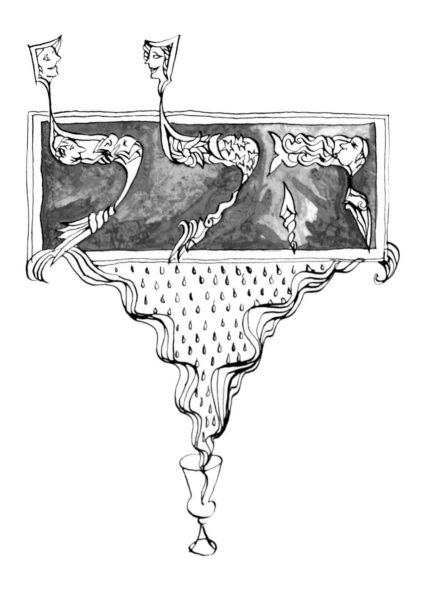

HALLEL

הַלֵּל

HALLEL
praise and meditation

Not to us, God, not to us,
but to Your Name give glory;
for the sake of Your kindness
and your truth! Why should
the nations say, "Where, now,
is their God? Our God is in heaven,
whatever He desires, He does!
Their idols are of silver and gold,
the work of human hands.
They have a mouth but cannot
speak; they have eyes but cannot
see. They have ears but cannot
hear; they have a nose but cannot
smell. Their hands do not feel;
feet, they cannot walk; no sound
comes from their throat!
Those that make them should
be like them, anyone that trusts
in them. (But) Israel! Trust in God!
He is their help and shield.
Those that fear God! Trust in God!
He is their help and shield.
House of Aharon! Trust in God!
He is their help and shield.
Those that fear God! Trust in God!
He is their help and shield.
(Psalms 115)

לֹא לָנוּ יְיָ לֹא לָנוּ כִּי לְשִׁמְךָ תֵּן
כָּבוֹד. עַל־חַסְדְּךָ עַל־אֲמִתֶּךָ:
לָמָּה יֹאמְרוּ הַגּוֹיִם. אַיֵּה־נָא
אֱלֹהֵיהֶם: וֵאלֹהֵינוּ בַשָּׁמָיִם. כֹּל
אֲשֶׁר־חָפֵץ עָשָׂה: עֲצַבֵּיהֶם כֶּסֶף
וְזָהָב. מַעֲשֵׂה יְדֵי אָדָם: פֶּה־לָהֶם
וְלֹא יְדַבֵּרוּ. עֵינַיִם לָהֶם וְלֹא
יִרְאוּ: אָזְנַיִם לָהֶם וְלֹא יִשְׁמָעוּ.
אַף לָהֶם וְלֹא יְרִיחוּן: יְדֵיהֶם
וְלֹא יְמִישׁוּן, רַגְלֵיהֶם וְלֹא
יְהַלֵּכוּ. לֹא־יֶהְגּוּ בִּגְרוֹנָם:
כְּמוֹהֶם יִהְיוּ עֹשֵׂיהֶם. כֹּל אֲשֶׁר־
בֹּטֵחַ בָּהֶם: יִשְׂרָאֵל בְּטַח בַּיְיָ.
עֶזְרָם וּמָגִנָּם הוּא: בֵּית אַהֲרֹן
בִּטְחוּ בַיְיָ. עֶזְרָם וּמָגִנָּם הוּא:
יִרְאֵי יְיָ בִּטְחוּ בַיְיָ. עֶזְרָם וּמָגִנָּם
הוּא:

THE ANGEL OF DEATH (EXODUS 12:12)

God will remember us, He will bless; He will bless the House of Israel, He will bless the House of Aharon. He will bless those that fear God, those small and great. May God add to you, to you and your children. You are blessed by God, the Maker of heaven and earth. The heavens are the heavens of God, but the earth He has given to man. The dead cannot praise God, nor those that go down in silence. But we will praise God, from now and forever, Hallelu-Yah!

(Psalms 115)

יְיָ זְכָרָנוּ יְבָרֵךְ. יְבָרֵךְ אֶת־בֵּית
יִשְׂרָאֵל, יְבָרֵךְ אֶת־בֵּית אַהֲרֹן:
יְבָרֵךְ יִרְאֵי יְיָ. הַקְּטַנִּים עִם־
הַגְּדֹלִים: יֹסֵף יְיָ עֲלֵיכֶם. עֲלֵיכֶם
וְעַל־בְּנֵיכֶם: בְּרוּכִים אַתֶּם לַיְיָ.
עֹשֵׂה שָׁמַיִם וָאָרֶץ: הַשָּׁמַיִם
שָׁמַיִם לַיְיָ. וְהָאָרֶץ נָתַן לִבְנֵי־
אָדָם: לֹא־הַמֵּתִים יְהַלְלוּ־יָהּ.
וְלֹא כָּל־יֹרְדֵי דוּמָה: וַאֲנַחְנוּ
נְבָרֵךְ יָהּ מֵעַתָּה וְעַד־עוֹלָם
הַלְלוּיָהּ:

I love God, for He hears my voice and my prayer. He has listened to me, therefore I will call to Him all my life. The ropes of death encircled me, the confines of the grave took hold of me, trouble and sorrow I found. (But) I called the Name of God: "O, God, save my soul!" God is King and righteous, God is full of compassion. God guards the fools; I was brought low, but He saved me. Return, my soul, to your rest; for God was good to you.

אָהַבְתִּי כִּי־יִשְׁמַע יְיָ. אֶת־קוֹלִי
תַּחֲנוּנָי: כִּי־הִטָּה אָזְנוֹ לִי. וּבְיָמַי
אֶקְרָא: אֲפָפוּנִי חֶבְלֵי־מָוֶת
וּמְצָרֵי שְׁאוֹל מְצָאוּנִי. צָרָה
וְיָגוֹן אֶמְצָא: וּבְשֵׁם־יְיָ אֶקְרָא.
אָנָּה יְיָ מַלְּטָה נַפְשִׁי: חַנּוּן יְיָ
וְצַדִּיק. וֵאלֹהֵינוּ מְרַחֵם: שֹׁמֵר
פְּתָאִים יְיָ. דַּלּוֹתִי וְלִי יְהוֹשִׁיעַ:
שׁוּבִי נַפְשִׁי לִמְנוּחָיְכִי. כִּי יְיָ
גָּמַל עָלָיְכִי:

You (God) delivered
my soul from death,
my eyes from tears,
my feet from stumbling.
I will walk before God
in the land of the living.
I had much faith, therefore
I spoke, though I deeply
suffered—when I said in my
panic, "All men are liars!"

How can I repay God for all
His kindness to me?
I will lift up the cup of salvation,
and call the Name of God.
My vows to God, I will fulfill,
in the presence of His people.
Precious in the eyes of God,
is the death of His saints.
Please, God I am Your servant;
I am Your servant, son of
Your maid; You have unlocked
my chains. I will sacrifice
to You thanksgiving offerings,
and in the Name of God
I will call. My vows to God
I will fulfill, in the presence of
His people; in the courtyards
of God's Holy Temple, in your
midst, Jerusalem, Hallelu-Yah!

(Psalms 116)

כִּי חִלַּצְתָּ נַפְשִׁי מִמָּוֶת. אֶת־
עֵינִי מִן־דִּמְעָה, אֶת־רַגְלִי מִדֶּחִי:
אֶתְהַלֵּךְ לִפְנֵי יְיָ. בְּאַרְצוֹת
הַחַיִּים: הֶאֱמַנְתִּי כִּי אֲדַבֵּר. אֲנִי
עָנִיתִי מְאֹד: אֲנִי אָמַרְתִּי
בְחָפְזִי כָּל הָאָדָם כֹּזֵב:

מָה־אָשִׁיב לַיְיָ. כָּל־תַּגְמוּלוֹהִי
עָלָי: כּוֹס־יְשׁוּעוֹת אֶשָּׂא. וּבְשֵׁם
יְיָ אֶקְרָא: נְדָרַי לַיְיָ אֲשַׁלֵּם.
נֶגְדָה־נָּא לְכָל־עַמּוֹ: יָקָר בְּעֵינֵי
יְיָ. הַמָּוְתָה לַחֲסִידָיו: אָנָּה יְיָ כִּי־
אֲנִי עַבְדֶּךָ. אֲנִי עַבְדְּךָ בֶּן־
אֲמָתֶךָ. פִּתַּחְתָּ לְמוֹסֵרָי: לְךָ
אֶזְבַּח זֶבַח תּוֹדָה. וּבְשֵׁם יְיָ
אֶקְרָא: נְדָרַי לַיְיָ אֲשַׁלֵּם. נֶגְדָה־
נָּא לְכָל עַמּוֹ: בְּחַצְרוֹת בֵּית יְיָ.
בְּתוֹכֵכִי יְרוּשָׁלָיִם הַלְלוּיָהּ:

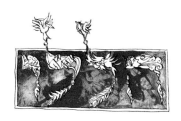

הַלְלוּ אֶת־יְיָ כָּל־גּוֹיִם. שַׁבְּחוּהוּ כָּל־הָאֻמִּים:
כִּי גָבַר עָלֵינוּ חַסְדּוֹ. וֶאֱמֶת־יְיָ לְעוֹלָם הַלְלוּיָהּ:

כִּי לְעוֹלָם חַסְדּוֹ:	הוֹדוּ לַיְיָ כִּי־טוֹב.
כִּי לְעוֹלָם חַסְדּוֹ:	יֹאמַר־נָא יִשְׂרָאֵל.
כִּי לְעוֹלָם חַסְדּוֹ:	יֹאמְרוּ נָא בֵית־אַהֲרֹן.
כִּי לְעוֹלָם חַסְדּוֹ:	יֹאמְרוּ נָא יִרְאֵי יְיָ.

מִן־הַמֵּצַר קָרָאתִי יָּהּ. עָנָנִי בַמֶּרְחַבְיָה: יְיָ לִי לֹא אִירָא.
מַה־יַּעֲשֶׂה לִי אָדָם: יְיָ לִי בְּעֹזְרָי. וַאֲנִי אֶרְאֶה בְשֹׂנְאָי:
טוֹב לַחֲסוֹת בַּיְיָ. מִבְּטֹחַ בָּאָדָם:
טוֹב לַחֲסוֹת בַּיְיָ. מִבְּטֹחַ בִּנְדִיבִים:
כָּל־גּוֹיִם סְבָבוּנִי. בְּשֵׁם יְיָ כִּי אֲמִילַם: סַבּוּנִי גַם־סְבָבוּנִי.
בְּשֵׁם יְיָ כִּי אֲמִילַם: סַבּוּנִי כִדְבֹרִים. דֹּעֲכוּ כְּאֵשׁ קוֹצִים.
בְּשֵׁם יְיָ כִּי אֲמִילַם: דָּחֹה דְחִיתַנִי לִנְפֹּל.

Praise God, all the nations;
praise Him, all peoples.
For His kindness overwhelmed us,
and God's truth is eternal.
Hallelu-Yah! (Psalms 117)

Give thanks to God, He is good: His kindness is forever.
Let Israel say: His kindness is forever.
Let the House of Aharon say: His kindness is forever.
Let those who fear God say: His kindness is forever.

In distress, I called to God;
He answered me extensively.
God is with me, I will have no fear,
what can man to do me?
God is with me to help me,
therefore, I can face my enemy.
It is better to rely on God,
than to trust in man.
It is better to rely on God,
than to trust in princes.
All nations surround me,
in God's Name I (can) destroy them. (Psalms 118)

They surround me,
they encircle me, in God's Name
I (can) destroy them.
They surround me like swarming
bees, they will burn out like fire
(consuming) thorns; with God's
Name I (can) destroy them.
They pushed me that I might
fall, but God assisted me.
God is my strength and song,
He is my salvation. The sound
of rejoicing and salvation
is in the tents of the righteous:
God's right hand prevails.
God's right hand is raised
triumphantly, God's right hand
prevails. I shall not die,
(but) I shall live and
relate the acts of God.
God made me suffer,
but He did not let me die.
Open for me the gates
of righteousness, I will
enter them and thank God.
This is the gate of God; the
righteous will enter through it.
I thank You, for You
answered me and were
my salvation. (repeat)
The stone despised
by the builders has become
the cornerstone. (repeat)
This is from God;
it is wonderful
in our eyes. (repeat)
This day, God has made,
we will rejoice and
be glad in Him. (repeat)

וַיְי עֶזְרָנִי: עָזִּי וְזִמְרָת יָהּ. וַיְהִי־לִי
לִישׁוּעָה: קוֹל רִנָּה וִישׁוּעָה
בְּאָהֳלֵי צַדִּיקִים. יְמִין יְיָ עֹשָׂה
חָיִל: יְמִין יְיָ רוֹמֵמָה. יְמִין יְיָ עֹשָׂה
חָיִל: לֹא־אָמוּת כִּי־אֶחְיֶה. וַאֲסַפֵּר
מַעֲשֵׂי־יָהּ: יַסֹּר יִסְּרַנִּי יָהּ. וְלַמָּוֶת
לֹא נְתָנָנִי: פִּתְחוּ לִי שַׁעֲרֵי־צֶדֶק.
אָבֹא־בָם אוֹדֶה יָהּ: זֶה הַשַּׁעַר
לַיְיָ. צַדִּיקִים יָבֹאוּ בוֹ:
אוֹדְךָ כִּי עֲנִיתָנִי.
וַתְּהִי־לִי לִישׁוּעָה:
אוֹדְךָ כִּי עֲנִיתָנִי.
וַתְּהִי־לִי לִישׁוּעָה:
אֶבֶן מָאֲסוּ הַבּוֹנִים.
הָיְתָה לְרֹאשׁ פִּנָּה:
אֶבֶן מָאֲסוּ הַבּוֹנִים.
הָיְתָה לְרֹאשׁ פִּנָּה:
מֵאֵת יְיָ הָיְתָה זֹּאת.
הִיא נִפְלָאת בְּעֵינֵינוּ:
מֵאֵת יְיָ הָיְתָה זֹּאת.
הִיא נִפְלָאת בְּעֵינֵינוּ:
זֶה הַיּוֹם עָשָׂה יְיָ.
נָגִילָה וְנִשְׂמְחָה בוֹ:
זֶה הַיּוֹם עָשָׂה יְיָ.
נָגִילָה וְנִשְׂמְחָה בוֹ:

God please save us!
God please save us!
God, please let us prosper!
God, please let us prosper!

אָנָּא יְיָ הוֹשִׁיעָה נָּא.
אָנָּא יְיָ הוֹשִׁיעָה נָּא.
אָנָּא יְיָ הַצְלִיחָה נָּא.
אָנָּא יְיָ הַצְלִיחָה נָּא:

Welcome to the one who comes
in the Name of God; we bless you
from the House of God. (repeat)
The Almighty is God and He
gives us light; bind the festival
(offering) with cords on
the corner of the altar. (repeat)
You are my God, and I will
thank You; (You are) my God
and I will exalt You. (repeat)
Give thanks to God, He is good;
His kindness is forever. (repeat)

(Psalms 118)

בָּרוּךְ הַבָּא בְּשֵׁם יְיָ. בֵּרַכְנוּכֶם
מִבֵּית יְיָ: בָּרוּךְ הַבָּא בְּשֵׁם יְיָ.
בֵּרַכְנוּכֶם מִבֵּית יְיָ:
אֵל יְיָ וַיָּאֶר לָנוּ. אִסְרוּ־חַג
בַּעֲבֹתִים עַד קַרְנוֹת הַמִּזְבֵּחַ:
אֵל יְיָ וַיָּאֶר לָנוּ. אִסְרוּ־חַג
בַּעֲבֹתִים עַד קַרְנוֹת הַמִּזְבֵּחַ:
אֵלִי אַתָּה וְאוֹדֶךָּ. אֱלֹהַי אֲרוֹמְמֶךָּ:
אֵלִי אַתָּה וְאוֹדֶךָּ. אֱלֹהַי אֲרוֹמְמֶךָּ:
הוֹדוּ לַיְיָ כִּי־טוֹב. כִּי לְעוֹלָם חַסְדּוֹ:
הוֹדוּ לַיְיָ כִּי־טוֹב. כִּי לְעוֹלָם חַסְדּוֹ:

All Your works shall praise You,
God, together with Your saints,
the righteous, who do Your will,
and Your people, Israel.
With song will they thank,
bless, praise, glorify, exalt,
revere, laud, sanctify, and crown
Your Name, our King, always.
To You it is good to give thanks,
and to Your Name it is proper
to sing praises, for from
the beginning of time
to eternity, You are God.

יְהַלְלוּךָ יְיָ אֱלֹהֵינוּ (עַל) כָּל־מַעֲשֶׂיךָ.
וַחֲסִידֶיךָ צַדִּיקִים עוֹשֵׂי רְצוֹנֶךָ וְכָל־
עַמְּךָ בֵּית יִשְׂרָאֵל בְּרִנָּה יוֹדוּ
וִיבָרְכוּ וִישַׁבְּחוּ וִיפָאֲרוּ וִירוֹמְמוּ
וְיַעֲרִיצוּ וְיַקְדִּישׁוּ וְיַמְלִיכוּ אֶת־
שִׁמְךָ מַלְכֵּנוּ, כִּי לְךָ טוֹב לְהוֹדוֹת,
וּלְשִׁמְךָ נָאֶה לְזַמֵּר, כִּי מֵעוֹלָם וְעַד
עוֹלָם אַתָּה אֵל:

הוֹדוּ לַיְיָ כִּי־טוֹב. כִּי לְעוֹלָם חַסְדּוֹ:

הוֹדוּ לֵאלֹהֵי הָאֱלֹהִים. כִּי לְעוֹלָם חַסְדּוֹ:

הוֹדוּ לַאֲדֹנֵי הָאֲדֹנִים. כִּי לְעוֹלָם חַסְדּוֹ:

לְעֹשֵׂה נִפְלָאוֹת גְּדֹלוֹת לְבַדּוֹ. כִּי לְעוֹלָם חַסְדּוֹ:

לְעֹשֵׂה הַשָּׁמַיִם בִּתְבוּנָה. כִּי לְעוֹלָם חַסְדּוֹ:

לְרוֹקַע הָאָרֶץ עַל הַמָּיִם. כִּי לְעוֹלָם חַסְדּוֹ:

לְעֹשֵׂה אוֹרִים גְּדֹלִים. כִּי לְעוֹלָם חַסְדּוֹ:

אֶת הַשֶּׁמֶשׁ לְמֶמְשֶׁלֶת בַּיּוֹם. כִּי לְעוֹלָם חַסְדּוֹ:

אֶת הַיָּרֵחַ וְכוֹכָבִים לְמֶמְשְׁלוֹת בַּלָּיְלָה. כִּי לְעוֹלָם חַסְדּוֹ:

לְמַכֵּה מִצְרַיִם בִּבְכוֹרֵיהֶם. כִּי לְעוֹלָם חַסְדּוֹ:

וַיּוֹצֵא יִשְׂרָאֵל מִתּוֹכָם. כִּי לְעוֹלָם חַסְדּוֹ:

בְּיָד חֲזָקָה וּבִזְרוֹעַ נְטוּיָה. כִּי לְעוֹלָם חַסְדּוֹ:

לְגֹזֵר יַם סוּף לִגְזָרִים. כִּי לְעוֹלָם חַסְדּוֹ:

וְהֶעֱבִיר יִשְׂרָאֵל בְּתוֹכוֹ. כִּי לְעוֹלָם חַסְדּוֹ:

וְנִעֵר פַּרְעֹה וְחֵילוֹ בְיַם־סוּף. כִּי לְעוֹלָם חַסְדּוֹ:

לְמוֹלִיךְ עַמּוֹ בַּמִּדְבָּר. כִּי לְעוֹלָם חַסְדּוֹ:

לְמַכֵּה מְלָכִים גְּדֹלִים. כִּי לְעוֹלָם חַסְדּוֹ:

Give thanks to God, He is good:	His Kindness is forever.
Give thanks to the God of gods:	His Kindness is forever.
Who alone does great wonders:	His Kindness is forever.
Who makes the heaven with understanding:	His Kindness is forever.
Who spreads the earth over the waters:	His Kindness is forever.
Who makes great lights:	His Kindness is forever.
The sun to rule by day:	His Kindness is forever.
The moon and the stars to rule by night:	His Kindness is forever.

Who struck the Egyptians through their firstborn:	His Kindness is forever.
Who removed Israel from their midst:	His Kindness is forever.
With a strong hand and outstretched arm:	His Kindness is forever.
Who divided the Red Sea into lanes:	His Kindness is forever.
Who brought Israel through:	His Kindness is forever.
Who cast Pharaoh and his army into the Red Sea:	His Kindness is forever.
Who led His people through the desert:	His Kindness is forever.
Who smote great kings:	His Kindness is forever.

(Psalms 136)

וַיַּהֲרֹג מְלָכִים אַדִּירִים.   כִּי לְעוֹלָם חַסְדּוֹ:
לְסִיחוֹן מֶלֶךְ הָאֱמֹרִי.   כִּי לְעוֹלָם חַסְדּוֹ:
וּלְעוֹג מֶלֶךְ הַבָּשָׁן.   כִּי לְעוֹלָם חַסְדּוֹ:
וְנָתַן אַרְצָם לְנַחֲלָה.   כִּי לְעוֹלָם חַסְדּוֹ:
נַחֲלָה לְיִשְׂרָאֵל עַבְדּוֹ.   כִּי לְעוֹלָם חַסְדּוֹ:
שֶׁבְּשִׁפְלֵנוּ זָכַר לָנוּ.   כִּי לְעוֹלָם חַסְדּוֹ:
וַיִּפְרְקֵנוּ מִצָּרֵינוּ.   כִּי לְעוֹלָם חַסְדּוֹ:
נוֹתֵן לֶחֶם לְכָל־בָּשָׂר.   כִּי לְעוֹלָם חַסְדּוֹ:
הוֹדוּ לְאֵל הַשָּׁמָיִם.   כִּי לְעוֹלָם חַסְדּוֹ:

Who slew mighty kings:	His Kindness is forever.
Sichon, the King of the Emorites:	His Kindness is forever.
And Og, the King of Bashan:	His Kindness is forever.
Who gave their land as heritage:	His Kindness is forever.
Heritage to Israel His servant:	His Kindness is forever.
Who remember us in our lowliness:	His Kindness is forever.
And redeemed us from our enemies:	His Kindness is forever.
He gives food to all flesh:	His Kindness is forever.
Thank God of heaven:	His Kindness is forever.

(Psalms 136)

The soul of all living beings
shall bless Your Name, God.
The spirit of all flesh
shall always praise and glorify
Your fame, our King, forever.
From all eternity You are God,
and except for You we have
no King, redeemer or helper.
He Who rescues, and redeems,
sustains and has compassion, in
every time of trouble and distress,
we have no King but You.
You are God of the first
and of the last,
God of all living creatures,
Master of all peoples,
Who is glorified
in a multitude of praises,
Who guides His world
with kindness
and His creatures
with compassion.

נִשְׁמַת כָּל־חַי תְּבָרֵךְ אֶת־
שִׁמְךָ, יְיָ אֱלֹהֵינוּ. וְרוּחַ
כָּל־בָּשָׂר תְּפָאֵר וּתְרוֹמֵם
זִכְרְךָ, מַלְכֵּנוּ, תָּמִיד. מִן־
הָעוֹלָם וְעַד־הָעוֹלָם אַתָּה
אֵל. וּמִבַּלְעָדֶיךָ אֵין לָנוּ
מֶלֶךְ, גּוֹאֵל וּמוֹשִׁיעַ, פּוֹדֶה
וּמַצִּיל, וּמְפַרְנֵס וּמְרַחֵם
בְּכָל־עֵת צָרָה וְצוּקָה. אֵין
לָנוּ מֶלֶךְ אֶלָּא אָתָּה:
אֱלֹהֵי הָרִאשׁוֹנִים
וְהָאַחֲרוֹנִים. אֱלוֹהַּ כָּל־
בְּרִיּוֹת, אֲדוֹן כָּל־תּוֹלָדוֹת,
הַמְהֻלָּל בְּרֹב הַתִּשְׁבָּחוֹת,
הַמְנַהֵג עוֹלָמוֹ בְּחֶסֶד
וּבְרִיּוֹתָיו בְּרַחֲמִים.

God does not slumber nor sleep.
He rouses the sleeping
and awakens those who slumber;
(He) makes the dumb speak,
frees the captives, supports
the fallen, raises the bent
and reveals the hidden.
To You alone we give thanks.
Were our mouths full with song
as the sea, our tongues full
with joy as the many waves,
our lips full with praise as broad
as the heavens, our eyes as bright
as the sun and the moon,
our hands outspread as the eagles
of the sky and our feet swift
as deer—we could never
sufficiently thank You, God,
God of our fathers, or bless
Your Name, for even one
of the countless thousands
upon thousands of good deeds,
miracles and wonders which You
did for our fathers and for us.
You delivered us from Egypt,
God, and redeemed us from
slavery. In hunger, You fed us;
in plenty, You provided for us.
From the sword, You spared us;
from the plague, You let us
escape; and from severe
and grievous diseases,
You preserved us.

וַיְיָ לֹא־יָנוּם וְלֹא־יִישָׁן. הַמְעוֹרֵר
יְשֵׁנִים וְהַמֵּקִיץ נִרְדָּמִים.
וְהַמֵּשִׂיחַ אִלְּמִים. וְהַמַּתִּיר
אֲסוּרִים וְהַסּוֹמֵךְ נוֹפְלִים
וְהַזּוֹקֵף כְּפוּפִים. לְךָ לְבַדְּךָ
אֲנַחְנוּ מוֹדִים: אִלּוּ פִינוּ מָלֵא
שִׁירָה כַּיָּם, וּלְשׁוֹנֵנוּ רִנָּה
כַּהֲמוֹן גַּלָּיו, וְשִׂפְתוֹתֵינוּ שֶׁבַח
כְּמֶרְחֲבֵי רָקִיעַ. וְעֵינֵינוּ
מְאִירוֹת כַּשֶּׁמֶשׁ וְכַיָּרֵחַ. וְיָדֵינוּ
פְרוּשׂוֹת כְּנִשְׁרֵי שָׁמָיִם.
וְרַגְלֵינוּ קַלּוֹת כָּאַיָּלוֹת. אֵין
אֲנַחְנוּ מַסְפִּיקִים לְהוֹדוֹת לְךָ, יְיָ
אֱלֹהֵינוּ וֵאלֹהֵי אֲבוֹתֵינוּ. וּלְבָרֵךְ
אֶת־שְׁמֶךָ. עַל־אַחַת מֵאֶלֶף אֶלֶף
אַלְפֵי אֲלָפִים וְרִבֵּי רְבָבוֹת
פְּעָמִים הַטּוֹבוֹת שֶׁעָשִׂיתָ עִם־
אֲבוֹתֵינוּ וְעִמָּנוּ: מִמִּצְרַיִם
גְּאַלְתָּנוּ, יְיָ אֱלֹהֵינוּ, וּמִבֵּית
עֲבָדִים פְּדִיתָנוּ. בְּרָעָב זַנְתָּנוּ
וּבְשָׂבָע כִּלְכַּלְתָּנוּ. מֵחֶרֶב
הִצַּלְתָּנוּ. וּמִדֶּבֶר מִלַּטְתָּנוּ.
וּמֵחֳלָיִם רָעִים וְנֶאֱמָנִים
דִּלִּיתָנוּ:

Until now Your compassion
has helped us, Your kindness
has not left us; please do
not abandon us, God forever.
Therefore, the limbs You gave us,
the spirit and soul which
You breathed into our nostrils,
and the tongue which You placed
in our mouth—all shall thank
and bless, praise and glorify,
exalt, revere, sanctify and crown
Your Name, our King.
Every mouth shall offer
to You thanks, every tongue
shall promise loyalty, every eye
shall look toward you, every knee
shall bend, all who stand shall
bow before You; all hearts shall
fear You; and man's innards
and thoughts shall sing praises
to Your Name, as it is written:
"All my bones shall say: 'God,
who is like You?' You help
the poor from those stronger
than he, the poor and needy from
the one who would rob him"
(Psalms 35:10). Who is like You?
Who is equal to You?
Who can be compared to You?
God Who is great, mighty,
and awesome; God
Who is most high, to Whom
heaven and earth belong.

עַד־הֵנָּה עֲזָרוּנוּ רַחֲמֶיךָ. וְלֹא־
עֲזָבוּנוּ חֲסָדֶיךָ. וְאַל־תִּטְּשֵׁנוּ, יְיָ
אֱלֹהֵינוּ, לָנֶצַח: עַל־כֵּן אֵבָרִים
שֶׁפִּלַּגְתָּ בָּנוּ. וְרוּחַ וּנְשָׁמָה
שֶׁנָּפַחְתָּ בְּאַפֵּינוּ. וְלָשׁוֹן אֲשֶׁר
שַׂמְתָּ בְּפִינוּ. הֵן הֵם יוֹדוּ
וִיבָרְכוּ וִישַׁבְּחוּ וִיפָאֲרוּ
וִירוֹמְמוּ וְיַעֲרִיצוּ וְיַקְדִּישׁוּ
וְיַמְלִיכוּ אֶת־שִׁמְךָ מַלְכֵּנוּ: כִּי
כָל־פֶּה לְךָ יוֹדֶה. וְכָל־לָשׁוֹן לְךָ
תִשָּׁבַע. וְכָל־בֶּרֶךְ לְךָ תִכְרַע.
וְכָל־קוֹמָה לְפָנֶיךָ תִשְׁתַּחֲוֶה.
וְכָל־לְבָבוֹת יִירָאוּךָ. וְכָל־קֶרֶב
וּכְלָיוֹת יְזַמְּרוּ לִשְׁמֶךָ. כַּדָּבָר
שֶׁכָּתוּב. כָּל־עַצְמוֹתַי תֹּאמַרְנָה,
יְיָ מִי כָמוֹךָ. מַצִּיל עָנִי מֵחָזָק
מִמֶּנּוּ, וְעָנִי וְאֶבְיוֹן מִגֹּזְלוֹ: מִי
יִדְמֶה־לָּךְ וּמִי יִשְׁוֶה־לָּךְ וּמִי
יַעֲרָךְ־לָךְ: הָאֵל הַגָּדוֹל הַגִּבּוֹר
וְהַנּוֹרָא, אֵל עֶלְיוֹן, קֹנֵה שָׁמַיִם
וָאָרֶץ:

THE PROPHET ELIJAH AND THE REVELATION (1 KINGS 19.2)

We shall adore, praise and glorify you and bless Your holy Name, as it is written: "Of David: My soul shall bless God, and my whole inner being shall bless His holy Name" (Psalms 103:1). The almighty! Mighty in Your strength; Great in the honor of your Name; Powerful forever and awesome in Your deeds! The King Who sits upon a high and lofty throne! He Who dwells forever, exalted and holy is His Name. It is written: "Rejoice you righteous in God; for the just, praise is good to Him" (Psalms 33:1). In the mouths of the just, You shall be exalted; by the lips of the righteous, You shall be blessed; by the tongues of the pious, You shall be sanctified; and among the holy, You shall be praised.

And in the congregations of the myriads of Your people Israel, with joy, Your Name, our King, shall be glorified in all generations. For this is the duty of all creatures: before You, our God, God of our fathers, to thank, praise, honor, glorify, exalt, adore, show gratitude, bless, raise high, and sing praises—even more than all the songs and praises of David the son of Yishai, Your chosen servant.

נְהַלֶּלְךָ וּנְשַׁבֵּחֲךָ וּנְפָאֶרְךָ וּנְבָרֵךְ אֶת־שֵׁם קָדְשֶׁךָ. כָּאָמוּר. לְדָוִד, בָּרְכִי נַפְשִׁי אֶת־יְיָ, וְכָל־קְרָבַי אֶת־שֵׁם קָדְשׁוֹ: הָאֵל בְּתַעֲצֻמוֹת עֻזֶּךָ. הַגָּדוֹל בִּכְבוֹד שְׁמֶךָ. הַגִּבּוֹר לָנֶצַח וְהַנּוֹרָא בְּנוֹרְאוֹתֶיךָ. הַמֶּלֶךְ הַיּוֹשֵׁב עַל־כִּסֵּא רָם וְנִשָּׂא: שׁוֹכֵן עַד, מָרוֹם וְקָדוֹשׁ שְׁמוֹ. וְכָתוּב. רַנְּנוּ צַדִּיקִים בַּייָ, לַיְשָׁרִים נָאוָה תְהִלָּה: בְּפִי יְשָׁרִים תִּתְהַלָּל. וּבְדִבְרֵי צַדִּיקִים תִּתְבָּרַךְ. וּבִלְשׁוֹן חֲסִידִים תִּתְרוֹמָם. וּבְקֶרֶב קְדוֹשִׁים תִּתְקַדָּשׁ:

וּבְמַקְהֲלוֹת רִבְבוֹת עַמְּךָ בֵּית יִשְׂרָאֵל, בְּרִנָּה יִתְפָּאַר שִׁמְךָ, מַלְכֵּנוּ, בְּכָל־דּוֹר וָדוֹר. שֶׁכֵּן חוֹבַת כָּל־הַיְצוּרִים, לְפָנֶיךָ, יְיָ אֱלֹהֵינוּ, וֵאלֹהֵי אֲבוֹתֵינוּ, לְהוֹדוֹת לְהַלֵּל לְשַׁבֵּחַ לְפָאֵר לְרוֹמֵם לְהַדֵּר לְבָרֵךְ לְעַלֵּה וּלְקַלֵּס עַל כָּל־דִּבְרֵי שִׁירוֹת וְתִשְׁבְּחוֹת דָּוִד בֶּן־יִשַׁי עַבְדְּךָ מְשִׁיחֶךָ:

יִשְׁתַּבַּח שִׁמְךָ לָעַד מַלְכֵּנוּ, הָאֵל הַמֶּלֶךְ הַגָּדוֹל וְהַקָּדוֹשׁ בַּשָּׁמַיִם וּבָאָרֶץ. כִּי לְךָ נָאֶה, יְיָ אֱלֹהֵינוּ וֵאלֹהֵי אֲבוֹתֵינוּ, שִׁיר וּשְׁבָחָה, הַלֵּל וְזִמְרָה, עֹז וּמֶמְשָׁלָה, נֶצַח גְּדֻלָּה וּגְבוּרָה, תְּהִלָּה וְתִפְאֶרֶת, קְדֻשָּׁה וּמַלְכוּת, בְּרָכוֹת וְהוֹדָאוֹת, מֵעַתָּה וְעַד־עוֹלָם: בָּרוּךְ אַתָּה יְיָ, אֵל מֶלֶךְ גָּדוֹל בַּתִּשְׁבָּחוֹת, אֵל הַהוֹדָאוֹת, אֲדוֹן הַנִּפְלָאוֹת, הַבּוֹחֵר בְּשִׁירֵי זִמְרָה, מֶלֶךְ אֵל חֵי הָעוֹלָמִים:

וּבְכֵן וַיְהִי בַּחֲצִי הַלַּיְלָה:
אָז רוֹב נִסִּים הִפְלֵאתָ בַּלַּיְלָה:
בְּרֹאשׁ אַשְׁמוּרוֹת זֶה הַלַּיְלָה:
גֵּר צֶדֶק נִצַּחְתּוֹ כְּנֶחֱלַק לוֹ לַיְלָה

וַיְהִי בַּחֲצִי הַלָּיְלָה:

דַּנְתָּ מֶלֶךְ גְּרָר בַּחֲלוֹם הַלַּיְלָה:
הִפְחַדְתָּ אֲרַמִּי בְּאֶמֶשׁ לַיְלָה:
וַיָּשַׂר יִשְׂרָאֵל לְמַלְאָךְ וַיּוּכַל לוֹ לַיְלָה

וַיְהִי בַּחֲצִי הַלָּיְלָה:

Therefore, may Your Name be praised forever, our King, God, Who is great and holy in the heavens and on earth. To You, God, God of our fathers, are song and praise, honor and hymns, strength and power, victory, greatness and might, praise and glory, holiness and sovereignty; blessings and thanksgiving to Your great and holy Name, from this world and in the World to Come—You are God. Blessed are You, God, King, great and praised in glory, God of thanksgiving, Master of wonders, Who creates all the souls, (Who is) Master of all works, Who chooses songs of praise—King, One (God), Life of all worlds.

ON THE FIRST NIGHT RECITE THE FOLLOWING:

It was at Midnight.

Many miracles You performed at night, at the beginning of the watch of this very night, the righteous convert (Avraham) triumphed when the night was divided for him:
It was at Midnight.

You judged the King of G'rar (Avimelech) during a dream at night, You frightened the Aramean (Lavan) in the dark of night, Israel (Yaakov) fought with an angel and overcame him by night:
It was at Midnight.

The firstborn of Egypt
You smote at midnight,
they did not find strength
upon arising at night, the army
of Charoshet (Sisera),
You swept away with
the stars of the night:
It was at Midnight.

The blasphemous (Sennacherib)
planned to rise against Your
desired (Jerusalem) but You
dried his (army's) corpse(s) at
night, Bel (Nevukhadnezzar's
idol) with its pedestal was
overturned in the darkness of
night, to the beloved (Daniel)
was revealed the visions of night:
It was at Midnight.

He (Belshatzar) who drank
from the Temple's vessels
was killed at night, He (Daniel)
who was rescued from the lion's
den, who revealed the dreams
of the night, the Aggagite
(Haman) nursed, hatred,
and wrote decrees at night:
It was at Midnight.

זֶרַע בְּכוֹרֵי פַתְרוֹם מָחַצְתָּ
בַּחֲצִי הַלָּיְלָה:
חֵילָם לֹא מָצְאוּ בְּקוּמָם בַּלָּיְלָה:
טִיסַת נְגִיד חֲרֹשֶׁת סִלִּיתָ
בְּכוֹכְבֵי לָיְלָה:
וַיְהִי בַּחֲצִי הַלָּיְלָה.

יָעַץ מְחָרֵף לְנוֹפֵף אִוּוּי הוֹבַשְׁתָּ
פְגָרָיו בַּלָּיְלָה:
כָּרַע בֵּל וּמַצָּבוֹ בְּאִישׁוֹן לָיְלָה
לְאִישׁ חֲמוּדוֹת נִגְלָה רַז חֲזוֹת
לָיְלָה:
וַיְהִי בַּחֲצִי הַלָּיְלָה:

מִשְׁתַּכֵּר בִּכְלֵי קֹדֶשׁ נֶהֱרַג בּוֹ
בַּלָּיְלָה:
נוֹשַׁע מִבּוֹר אֲרָיוֹת פּוֹתֵר
בְּעָתוּתֵי לָיְלָה:
שִׂנְאָה נָטַר אֲגָגִי וְכָתַב סְפָרִים
לָיְלָה:
וַיְהִי בַּחֲצִי הַלָּיְלָה:

You subdued him when You disturbed his (Achashveirosh) sleep at night, You will crush evil (Edom) to help those who ask the night-watchman, "How goes the night?" He will cry out like a watchman, and say "Morning comes and also night":
It was at Midnight.

Near is the Day (of the Mashiach) that is neither day nor night, most high! Make known that day is Yours and so is the night, appoint guards for Your city, all the day and all the night, light up as day, the darkness of the night:
It was at Midnight.

עוֹרַרְתָּ נִצְחֲךָ עָלָיו בְּנֶדֶד שְׁנַת לַיְלָה:

פּוּרָה תִדְרוֹךְ לְשׁוֹמֵר מַה מִלַּיְלָה:

צָרַח כַּשּׁוֹמֵר וְשָׂח אָתָא בֹקֶר וְגַם לַיְלָה:

וַיְהִי בַּחֲצִי הַלַּיְלָה:

קָרֵב יוֹם אֲשֶׁר הוּא לֹא יוֹם וְלֹא לַיְלָה:

רָם הוֹדַע כִּי לְךָ הַיּוֹם אַף לְךָ הַלַּיְלָה:

שׁוֹמְרִים הַפְקֵד לְעִירְךָ כָּל הַיּוֹם וְכָל הַלַּיְלָה:

תָּאִיר כְּאוֹר יוֹם חֶשְׁכַּת לַיְלָה:

וַיְהִי בַּחֲצִי הַלַּיְלָה:

וּבְכֵן וַאֲמַרְתֶּם זֶבַח פֶּסַח:

בַּפֶּסַח: אֹמֶץ גְּבוּרוֹתֶיךָ הִפְלֵאתָ

פֶּסַח: בְּרֹאשׁ כָּל מוֹעֲדוֹת נִשֵּׂאתָ

פֶּסַח: גִּלִּיתָ לְאֶזְרָחִי חֲצוֹת לֵיל

וַאֲמַרְתֶּם זֶבַח פֶּסַח:

בַּפֶּסַח: דְּלָתָיו דָּפַקְתָּ כְּחֹם הַיּוֹם

בַּפֶּסַח: הִסְעִיד נוֹצְצִים עֻגוֹת מַצּוֹת

פֶּסַח: וְאֶל הַבָּקָר רָץ זֵכֶר לְשׁוֹר עֵרֶךְ

וַאֲמַרְתֶּם זֶבַח פֶּסַח.

ON THE SECOND NIGHT RECITE THE FOLLOWING:

And say: The Pesach Feast!

You displayed Your mighty
powers on Pesach, first of all
festivals You elevated the Pesach,
to Ezrachi (Avraham) You
revealed the coming
midnight of Pesach;
And say: The Pesach Feast!

You knocked at his (Avraham)
door in the day's heat on Pesach,
He fed the angels with
matzah-cakes on Pesach,
He ran to the herds in memory
of the ox of Pesach;
And say: The Pesach Feast!

זָעֲמוּ סְדוֹמִים וְלֹהֲטוּ בָאֵשׁ בַּפֶּסַח:
חֻלַּץ לוֹט מֵהֶם וּמַצּוֹת אָפָה בְּקֵץ פֶּסַח:
טֵאטֵאתָ אַדְמַת מֹף וְנֹף בְּעָבְרְךָ בַּפֶּסַח:
וַאֲמַרְתֶּם זֶבַח פֶּסַח:

יָהּ, רֹאשׁ כָּל אוֹן מָחַצְתָּ בְּלֵיל שִׁמּוּר פֶּסַח:
כַּבִּיר עַל בֵּן בְּכוֹר פָּסַחְתָּ בְּדַם פֶּסַח:
לְבִלְתִּי תֵת מַשְׁחִית לָבֹא בִּפְתָחַי בַּפֶּסַח:
וַאֲמַרְתֶּם זֶבַח פֶּסַח:

The Sodomites angered (God)
and were destroyed by fire
on Pesach, Lot was saved and
he baked matzot on Pesach,
You swept clean the soil of Egypt
when You passed over on Pesach;
And say: The Pesach Feast!

You smote the firstborn on
the night of Pesach, Mighty One!
You passed over the firstborn
(the Jews) because of the blood
of Pesach, not to let
the destroying angel enter
my door on Pesach;
And say: The Pesach Feast!

מִסְגֶּרֶת סֻגְּרָה בְּעִתּוֹתֵי   פֶּסַח:

נִשְׁמְדָה מִדְיָן בִּצְלִיל שְׂעוֹרֵי עֹמֶר   פֶּסַח:

שֹׂרְפוּ מִשְׁמַנֵּי פוּל וְלוּד בִּיקַד יְקוֹד   פֶּסַח:

וַאֲמַרְתֶּם זֶבַח פֶּסַח:

עוֹד הַיּוֹם בְּנֹב לַעֲמוֹד, עַד גָּעָה עוֹנַת   פֶּסַח:

פַּס יָד כָּתְבָה לְקַעֲקֵעַ צוּל   בְּפֶסַח:

צָפֹה הַצָּפִית עָרוֹךְ הַשֻּׁלְחָן   בְּפֶסַח:

וַאֲמַרְתֶּם זֶבַח פֶּסַח:

The walled city (Jerico) was
besieged on Pesach, Midian
was destroyed (by Gideon)
with the barley offering
from the Omer on Pesach,
Put and Lud were consumed
in a great fire on Pesach,
And say: The Pesach Feast!

The day of Now (Sennacherib)
stood waiting for Pesach,
the Hand wrote on the wall (for
Belshatzar), making a shadow on
Pesach, the watch was prepared,
the table spread on Pesach;
And say: The Pesach Feast!

קָהָל כִּנְּסָה הֲדַסָּה צוֹם לְשַׁלֵּשׁ בַּפֶּסַח:
רֹאשׁ מִבֵּית רָשָׁע מָחַצְתָּ בְּעֵץ חֲמִשִּׁים בַּפֶּסַח:
שְׁתֵּי אֵלֶּה רֶגַע, תָּבִיא לְעוּצִית בַּפֶּסַח:
תָּעֹז יָדְךָ וְתָרוּם יְמִינְךָ כְּלֵיל הִתְקַדֵּשׁ חַג פֶּסַח:
וַאֲמַרְתֶּם זֶבַח פֶּסַח:

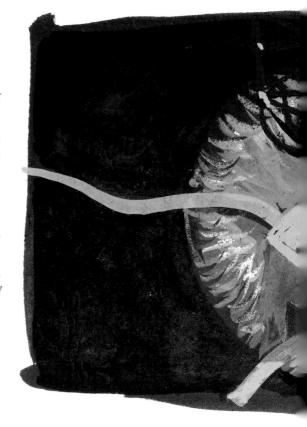

Hadassah (Esther) gathered
a congregation for a three-day
fast on Pesach, the head of
the evil house (Haman) was
hung on a fifty-cubit gallows
on Pesach, punishments
will be visited upon the wicked
kingdom Utzis (Edom)
on Pesach, may Your hand
be strong, Your right arm raised,
as on the night when You
sanctified the Festival of Pesach;
And say: The Pesach Feast!

To Him praise is due!
To Him praise is fitting!

Mighty in His Kingdom,
Chosen by right,
His armies say to Him:
To You and only to You;
to You, because it is Yours;
to You only, only Yours;
Yours, God, is the kingdom.
To Him praise is due!
To Him praise is fitting! (chorus:)

Famous in His kingdom,
glorious by right,
His good ones say to him:
(chorus:)

Pure in His kingdom,
powerful by right,
His servants say to Him:
(chorus:)

Alone in His kingdom,
strong by right,
His learned say to Him:
(chorus:)

Ruling in His kingdom,
awesome by right,
His surrounding (hosts) say to Him:
(chorus:)

כִּי לוֹ נָאֶה, כִּי לוֹ יָאֶה:

אַדִּיר בִּמְלוּכָה. בָּחוּר כַּהֲלָכָה.
גְּדוּדָיו יֹאמְרוּ לוֹ. לְךָ וּלְךָ. לְךָ כִּי
לְךָ, לְךָ אַף לְךָ. לְךָ יְיָ הַמַּמְלָכָה:
כִּי לוֹ נָאֶה, כִּי לוֹ יָאֶה:

דָּגוּל בִּמְלוּכָה. הָדוּר כַּהֲלָכָה.
וָתִיקָיו יֹאמְרוּ לוֹ. לְךָ וּלְךָ. לְךָ כִּי
לְךָ, לְךָ אַף לְךָ. לְךָ יְיָ הַמַּמְלָכָה:
כִּי לוֹ נָאֶה, כִּי לוֹ יָאֶה:

זַכַּאי בִּמְלוּכָה. חָסִין כַּהֲלָכָה.
טַפְסְרָיו יֹאמְרוּ לוֹ. לְךָ וּלְךָ. לְךָ
כִּי לְךָ. לְךָ אַף לְךָ, לְךָ יְיָ
הַמַּמְלָכָה:
כִּי לוֹ נָאֶה, כִּי לוֹ יָאֶה:

יָחִיד בִּמְלוּכָה. כַּבִּיר כַּהֲלָכָה.
לִמּוּדָיו יֹאמְרוּ לוֹ. לְךָ וּלְךָ, לְךָ כִּי
לְךָ, לְךָ אַף לְךָ. לְךָ יְיָ הַמַּמְלָכָה:
כִּי לוֹ נָאֶה, כִּי לוֹ יָאֶה:

מָרוֹם בִּמְלוּכָה. נוֹרָא כַּהֲלָכָה.
סְבִיבָיו יֹאמְרוּ לוֹ. לְךָ וּלְךָ. לְךָ כִּי
לְךָ, לְךָ אַף לְךָ. לְךָ יְיָ הַמַּמְלָכָה:
כִּי לוֹ נָאֶה, כִּי לוֹ יָאֶה:

עָנָו בִּמְלוּכָה. פּוֹדֶה כַּהֲלָכָה.
צַדִּיקָיו יֹאמְרוּ לוֹ. לְךָ וּלְךָ. לְךָ כִּי
לְךָ, לְךָ אַף לְךָ. לְךָ יְיָ הַמַּמְלָכָה:
כִּי לוֹ נָאֶה, כִּי לוֹ יָאֶה:

קָדוֹשׁ בִּמְלוּכָה. רַחוּם כַּהֲלָכָה.
שִׁנְאַנָּיו יֹאמְרוּ לוֹ. לְךָ וּלְךָ. לְךָ כִּי
לְךָ, לְךָ אַף לְךָ. לְךָ יְיָ הַמַּמְלָכָה:
כִּי לוֹ נָאֶה, כִּי לוֹ יָאֶה:

תַּקִּיף בִּמְלוּכָה. תּוֹמֵךְ כַּהֲלָכָה.
תְּמִימָיו יֹאמְרוּ לוֹ. לְךָ וּלְךָ, לְךָ כִּי
לְךָ. לְךָ אַף לְךָ, לְךָ יְיָ הַמַּמְלָכָה:
כִּי לוֹ נָאֶה, כִּי לוֹ יָאֶה:

לְשָׁנָה הַבָּאָה בִּירוּשָׁלָיִם:

בָּרוּךְ אַתָּה יְיָ אֱלֹהֵינוּ מֶלֶךְ
הָעוֹלָם בּוֹרֵא פְּרִי הַגָּפֶן:

Modest in His kingdom,
redeemer by right,
His righteous say to Him:
(chorus:)

Holy in His kingdom,
merciful by right,
His angels say to Him:
(chorus:)

Powerful in His kingdom,
supporter by right,
His perfect ones say to Him:
(chorus:)

THRICE:

Next year in Jerusalem.

THE BLESSING OVER THE FOURTH
AND LAST CUP IS RECITED:

Blessed are you, God,
King of the universe,
Who creates the fruit of the vine.

THEN DRINK THIS ENTIRE CUP
WHILE RECLINING TO THE LEFT SIDE.
AFTER DRINKING THE FOURTH CUP,
THE FOLLOWING BLESSING IS RECITED:

Blessed are You, God,
King of the universe,
for the vine, the fruit of the vine,
and for the produce of the field;
for the desirable, good and
spacious land that You desired
and gave our forefathers
as a heritage, to eat of its fruit
and be satisfied with its good.
Have mercy, we beg You, God,
on Israel, Your people;
on Jerusalem, Your city; on Zion,
home of Your glory;
on Your altar, and Your Temple.
Rebuild Jerusalem, the city
of holiness, speedily in our days;
bring us into it; make us
happy with its rebuilding; let us
eat from its fruit and be satisfied
with its good; and we will bless
You upon it in holiness and purity.
(On Shabbat: be pleased and
strengthen us on this Shabbat.)
Give us happiness on this
Festival of matzot; for You,
God, are good, and do good
to all, and we thank You for the
land and for the fruit of the vine.
Blessed are You, God, for the
Land and for the fruit of the vine.

בָּרוּךְ אַתָּה יְיָ אֱלֹהֵינוּ מֶלֶךְ
הָעוֹלָם עַל הַגֶּפֶן וְעַל פְּרִי הַגֶּפֶן
וְעַל תְּנוּבַת הַשָּׂדֶה וְעַל אֶרֶץ
חֶמְדָּה טוֹבָה וּרְחָבָה שֶׁרָצִיתָ
וְהִנְחַלְתָּ לַאֲבוֹתֵינוּ, לֶאֱכוֹל
מִפִּרְיָהּ וְלִשְׂבּוֹעַ מִטּוּבָהּ. רַחֶם,
יְיָ אֱלֹהֵינוּ, עַל יִשְׂרָאֵל עַמֶּךְ,
וְעַל יְרוּשָׁלַיִם עִירֶךְ, וְעַל צִיּוֹן
מִשְׁכַּן כְּבוֹדֶךְ וְעַל מִזְבְּחֶךְ וְעַל
הֵיכָלֶךְ. וּבְנֵה יְרוּשָׁלַיִם עִיר
הַקֹּדֶשׁ בִּמְהֵרָה בְיָמֵינוּ וְהַעֲלֵנוּ
לְתוֹכָהּ וְשַׂמְּחֵנוּ בְּבִנְיָנָהּ,
וְנֹאכַל מִפִּרְיָהּ וְנִשְׂבַּע מִטּוּבָהּ
וּנְבָרֶכְךָ עָלֶיהָ בִּקְדֻשָּׁה
וּבְטָהֳרָה. (וּרְצֵה וְהַחֲלִיצֵנוּ
בְּיוֹם הַשַּׁבָּת הַזֶּה) וְשַׂמְּחֵנוּ
בְּיוֹם חַג הַמַּצּוֹת הַזֶּה. כִּי אַתָּה
יְיָ טוֹב וּמֵטִיב לַכֹּל וְנוֹדֶה לְּךָ
עַל הָאָרֶץ וְעַל פְּרִי הַגֶּפֶן. בָּרוּךְ
אַתָּה יְיָ עַל הָאָרֶץ וְעַל פְּרִי
הַגֶּפֶן:

HALLEL
praise and meditation

Beside the text of the psalms and prayers that are recited in this part of the Seder, the important ritual is opening the door for the Elijah the prophet. The Seder begins as it ended, with a greeting. But here it is not the stranger and the poor who are expected. It is the prophet, the one of whom it is said that he is present at every circumcision, an immortal, who can assume the aspect of a prince or a beggar, and who is always there, at the right moment, to help and save.

The prophet Malachi writes: "Behold I will send you Elijah the prophet before the coming of the great and dreadful day of the Lord. And he shall turn the heart of the fathers to the children and the heart of the children to the fathers, lest I come and strike the earth with a curse." (3,23-24)

Elijah is also the prophet of reconciliation between the generations, and therefore his presence is central on the Seder night. A night of transmission, the Seder is the time of mutual rediscovery between the generations, and this is the goal that the participants in the Seder should attain when they have finished reading the Haggadah.

Essentially, Elijah the prophet is also a particular way of perceiving the divine, of living the Revelation.

When Elijah fled from Jezabel, the text of the Book of Kings describes the episode when the prophet found himself on Mount Horev. He passes the night in a cave, and God addresses him:

"And he said: 'Go forth and stand upon the mount before the Lord.' And behold the Lord passed by, and a great and strong wind rent the mountains, and broke the rocks in pieces before the Lord; but the Lord was not in the wind; and after the wind an earthquake; but the Lord was not in the earthquake; and after the earthquake a fire; and after the fire a still small voice. And so it was when Elijah heard it, that he wrapped his face in his mantle and went out and stood in the entrance of the cave. And behold there came a voice unto him, and said, What are you doing here, Elijah?" (1 Kings 19:11-13)

"A Revelation took place here, the most surprising of revelations, because it is the barest. It is a revelation that voids itself, nullifies, denies glory and power, renounces the grandiose. A revelation of nothing, of infinite discretion. Blow after blow explodes: a storm, an earthquake, a violent fire. Each time, it is stated that God is not present. Spectacular events are mentioned merely to be rejected, denounced as an illusion, even fakery. Three formidable blows resound for nothing. Rather, could it be that these are the three blows to announce the rising of the curtain, calling *upon the spectator to pay attention, to concentrate, to listen vigilantly? For indeed it is then, only then, that something happens, an unheard of 'I don't know what.'" (Translated from Sylvie Germain,* Les échos du silence, *DDB, p. 46.)*

What the ritual and the cup of Elijah seek to teach us is that the Seder closes upon a return to oneself in calm and serenity, in meditation and silence. After all the display and the demonstrations of the Seder night, where both children and adults have played hide and seek with the visible and the invisible, everything happens as if the evening were only just beginning. That is why one opens the door as at the beginning of the Seder.

Now comes the true Revelation, "a still small voice."

One must have sharpened one's hearing, to be led to the absolute level of attention, to become capable of perceiving such a tenuous breath. One must have sounded oneself, have explored oneself in the darkest places of consciousness, to the furthest of thoughts, to have made the circuit of one's inner domain many times, in constantly growing but nevertheless tightening circles, so as to attain the intimate desert of self-forgetfulness, to be able to be stroked lightly, touched, visited by such an inaudible sigh.

At the limits of Elijah's thought, wearied by walking and by fasting, purified by forty days and nights in the desert, a sigh passes. A thread of silence that barely vibrates, and that has already gone away. God. (ibid.)

Part Fourteen

NIRTZAH

נִרְצָה

NIRTZAH

ending of the ceremony

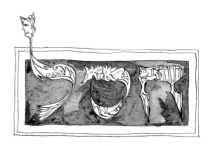

חֲסַל סִדּוּר פֶּסַח כְּהִלְכָתוֹ. כְּכָל מִשְׁפָּטוֹ וְחֻקָּתוֹ:
כַּאֲשֶׁר זָכִינוּ לְסַדֵּר אוֹתוֹ. כֵּן נִזְכֶּה לַעֲשׂוֹתוֹ:
זָךְ שׁוֹכֵן מְעוֹנָה. קוֹמֵם קְהַל מִי מָנָה:
קָרֵב נַהֵל נִטְעֵי כַנָּה. פְּדוּיִם לְצִיּוֹן בְּרִנָּה:

The Seder is completed in accordance with its laws,

With all its statutes and symbols;

Just as we merited to arrange it, so may we merit to fulfill it.

Pure One, Who dwells on high,

Raise up the countless congregation soon,

Guide the plantings of Your vineyard,

Redeemed, to Zion, in joyous song.

Mighty is He, Mighty is He
*He will rebuilt His Temple soon,
speedily, in our days, soon.
God, rebuild, God, rebuild
Your Temple soon. (chorus:)*

אַדִּיר הוּא.
יִבְנֶה בֵיתוֹ בְּקָרוֹב. בִּמְהֵרָה
בִּמְהֵרָה. בְּיָמֵינוּ בְּקָרוֹב. אֵל
בְּנֵה. בְּנֵה בֵיתְךָ בְּקָרוֹב:

Chosen is He,
Great is He,
Famous is He
(chorus:)

Brilliant is He,
Faithful is He,
Faultless is He
(chorus:)

Meritorious is He,
Pure is He,
Alone is He
(chorus:)

Sturdy is He,
Learned is He,
Royal is He
(chorus:)

בָּחוּר הוּא. גָּדוֹל הוּא. דָּגוּל הוּא.
יִבְנֶה בֵיתוֹ בְּקָרוֹב. בִּמְהֵרָה
בִּמְהֵרָה. בְּיָמֵינוּ בְּקָרוֹב. אֵל
בְּנֵה. אֵל בְּנֵה. בְּנֵה בֵיתְךָ
בְּקָרוֹב:

הָדוּר הוּא. וָתִיק הוּא. זַכַּאי הוּא.
יִבְנֶה בֵיתוֹ בְּקָרוֹב. בִּמְהֵרָה
בִּמְהֵרָה. בְּיָמֵינוּ בְּקָרוֹב. אֵל
בְּנֵה. אֵל בְּנֵה. בְּנֵה בֵיתְךָ
בְּקָרוֹב:

חָסִיד הוּא. טָהוֹר הוּא. יָחִיד
הוּא. יִבְנֶה בֵיתוֹ בְּקָרוֹב.
בִּמְהֵרָה בִּמְהֵרָה. בְּיָמֵינוּ בְּקָרוֹב.
אֵל בְּנֵה. אֵל בְּנֵה. בְּנֵה בֵיתְךָ
בְּקָרוֹב:

כַּבִּיר הוּא. לָמוּד הוּא. מֶלֶךְ הוּא.
יִבְנֶה בֵיתוֹ בְּקָרוֹב. בִּמְהֵרָה
בִּמְהֵרָה. בְּיָמֵינוּ בְּקָרוֹב. אֵל
בְּנֵה. אֵל בְּנֵה. בְּנֵה בֵיתְךָ
בְּקָרוֹב:

Awesome is He,
Highest is He,
Strong is He,
(chorus)

Redeemer is He,
Righteous is He,
Holy is He
(chorus:)

Merciful is He,
Almighty is He,
Powerful is He
(chorus:)

נָאוֹר הוּא. סַגִּיב הוּא. עִזּוּז הוּא.
יִבְנֶה בֵיתוֹ בְּקָרוֹב. בִּמְהֵרָה
בִּמְהֵרָה. בְּיָמֵינוּ בְּקָרוֹב. אֵל
בְּנֵה. אֵל בְּנֵה. בְּנֵה בֵיתְךָ
בְּקָרוֹב:

פּוֹדֶה הוּא. צַדִּיק הוּא. קָדוֹשׁ
הוּא. יִבְנֶה בֵיתוֹ בְּקָרוֹב.
בִּמְהֵרָה בִּמְהֵרָה. בְּיָמֵינוּ בְּקָרוֹב.
אֵל בְּנֵה. אֵל בְּנֵה. בְּנֵה בֵיתְךָ
בְּקָרוֹב:

רַחוּם הוּא. שַׁדַּי הוּא. תַּקִּיף הוּא.
יִבְנֶה בֵיתוֹ בְּקָרוֹב. בִּמְהֵרָה
בִּמְהֵרָה. בְּיָמֵינוּ בְּקָרוֹב. אֵל
בְּנֵה. אֵל בְּנֵה. בְּנֵה בֵיתְךָ
בְּקָרוֹב:

ONE THE 16TH DAY OF NISSAN,
THE SECOND EVENING OF PESACH,
ONE BEGINS TO COUNT THE OMER.
OUTSIDE THE HOLY LAND THIS TAKES PLACE
ON THE NIGHT OF THE SECOND SEDER.
SOME BEGIN COUNTING IN THE SYNAGOGUE
AT THE CONCLUSION OF THE EVENING SERVICE,
BUT, ACCORDING TO THE ARI,
ONE SHOULD COUNT AT THE SEDER,
PRIOR TO "WHO KNOWS ONE." PRIOR THE
COUNTING THE OMER THE FOLLOWING IS SAID:

Counting of the Omer.

Blessed are You, God,
King of the universe,
Who has made us holy with
His mitzvot, and commanded
us to Count the Omer.

Today is
one day of the Omer.

Let it be your will, God,
our Lord, and God of our fathers,
to build the Holy Temple,
speedily in our days, and let us
enter to our part of Your Torah.

בָּרוּךְ אַתָּה יְיָ, אֱלֹהֵינוּ
מֶלֶךְ הָעוֹלָם, אֲשֶׁר
קִדְּשָׁנוּ בְּמִצְוֹתָיו וְצִוָּנוּ
עַל סְפִירַת הָעֹמֶר:

הַיּוֹם יוֹם אֶחָד לָעֹמֶר:

יְהִי רָצוֹן מִלְּפָנֶיךָ יְיָ אֱלֹהֵינוּ
וֵאלֹהֵי אֲבוֹתֵינוּ שֶׁיִּבָּנֶה בֵּית
הַמִּקְדָּשׁ בִּמְהֵרָה בְּיָמֵינוּ וְתֵן
חֶלְקֵנוּ בְּתוֹרָתֶךָ:

Ehad mi yodea

אֶחָד מִי יוֹדֵעַ. אֶחָד אֲנִי יוֹדֵעַ:
אֶחָד אֱלֹהֵינוּ שֶׁבַּשָּׁמַיִם וּבָאָרֶץ.

Who knows one?
I know one: One is our God,
in heaven and on earth.

שְׁנַיִם מִי יוֹדֵעַ. שְׁנַיִם אֲנִי
יוֹדֵעַ: שְׁנֵי לֻחוֹת הַבְּרִית, אֶחָד
אֱלֹהֵינוּ שֶׁבַּשָּׁמַיִם וּבָאָרֶץ.

Who knows two?
I know two: two are the Tablets;
one is our God,
in heaven and on earth.

שְׁלֹשָׁה מִי יוֹדֵעַ. שְׁלֹשָׁה אֲנִי
יוֹדֵעַ: שְׁלֹשָׁה אָבוֹת, שְׁנֵי לֻחוֹת
הַבְּרִית, אֶחָד אֱלֹהֵינוּ
שֶׁבַּשָּׁמַיִם וּבָאָרֶץ.

Who knows three?
I know three: three are the
Patriarchs; two are the Tablets;
one is our God,
in heaven and on earth.

אַרְבַּע מִי יוֹדֵעַ. אַרְבַּע אֲנִי
יוֹדֵעַ: אַרְבַּע אִמָּהוֹת, שְׁלֹשָׁה
אָבוֹת, שְׁנֵי לֻחוֹת הַבְּרִית, אֶחָד
אֱלֹהֵינוּ שֶׁבַּשָּׁמַיִם וּבָאָרֶץ.

Who knows four?
I know four: four are the
Matriarchs; three are the
Patriarchs; two are the Tablets;
one is our God,
in heaven and on earth.

חֲמִשָּׁה מִי יוֹדֵעַ. חֲמִשָּׁה אֲנִי
יוֹדֵעַ: חֲמִשָּׁה חוּמְשֵׁי תוֹרָה,
אַרְבַּע אִמָּהוֹת, שְׁלֹשָׁה אָבוֹת,
שְׁנֵי לֻחוֹת הַבְּרִית, אֶחָד
אֱלֹהֵינוּ שֶׁבַּשָּׁמַיִם וּבָאָרֶץ.

Who knows five?
I know five: five are the Books
of Torah; four are the
Matriarchs; three are the
Patriarchs; two are the Tablets;
one is our God,
in heaven and on earth.

THE NIGHT OF THE TENT (GENESIS 15:5)

שִׁשָּׁה מִי יוֹדֵעַ. שִׁשָּׁה אֲנִי יוֹדֵעַ: שִׁשָּׁה סִדְרֵי מִשְׁנָה, חֲמִשָּׁה חוּמְשֵׁי תוֹרָה, אַרְבַּע אִמָּהוֹת, שְׁלֹשָׁה אָבוֹת, שְׁנֵי לֻחוֹת הַבְּרִית, אֶחָד אֱלֹהֵינוּ שֶׁבַּשָּׁמַיִם וּבָאָרֶץ.

Who knows six?
I know six: six are the Orders
of Mishnah; five are the Books
of Torah; four are the
Matriarchs; three are the
Patriarchs; two are the Tablets;
one is our God,
in heaven and on earth.

שִׁבְעָה מִי יוֹדֵעַ. שִׁבְעָה אֲנִי יוֹדֵעַ: שִׁבְעָה יְמֵי שַׁבַּתָּא, שִׁשָּׁה סִדְרֵי מִשְׁנָה, חֲמִשָּׁה חוּמְשֵׁי תוֹרָה, אַרְבַּע אִמָּהוֹת, שְׁלֹשָׁה אָבוֹת, שְׁנֵי לֻחוֹת הַבְּרִית, אֶחָד אֱלֹהֵינוּ שֶׁבַּשָּׁמַיִם וּבָאָרֶץ.

Who knows seven?
I know seven: seven are the days
of the week; six are the Orders
of Mishnah; five are the Books
of Torah; four are the
Matriarchs; three are the
Patriarchs; two are the Tablets;
one is our God,
in heaven and on earth.

Who knows eight?
I know eight: eight are the days
until circumcision; seven are
the days of the week; six are
the Orders of Mishnah; five are
the Books of Torah; four are
the Matriarchs; three are the
Patriarchs; two are the Tablets;
one is our God,
in heaven and on earth.

שְׁמוֹנָה מִי יוֹדֵעַ. שְׁמוֹנָה אֲנִי יוֹדֵעַ: שְׁמוֹנָה יְמֵי מִילָה, שִׁבְעָה יְמֵי שַׁבַּתָּא, שִׁשָּׁה סִדְרֵי מִשְׁנָה, חֲמִשָּׁה חוּמְשֵׁי תוֹרָה, אַרְבַּע אִמָּהוֹת, שְׁלֹשָׁה אָבוֹת, שְׁנֵי לֻחוֹת הַבְּרִית, אֶחָד אֱלֹהֵינוּ שֶׁבַּשָּׁמַיִם וּבָאָרֶץ.

Who knows nine?
I know nine: nine are the
months of pregnancy; eight
are the days until circumcision;
seven are the days of the week;
six are the Orders of Mishnah;
five are the Books of Torah; four
are the Matriarchs; three are the
Patriarchs; two are the Tablets;
one is our God,
in heaven and on earth.

תִּשְׁעָה מִי יוֹדֵעַ. תִּשְׁעָה אֲנִי יוֹדֵעַ: תִּשְׁעָה יַרְחֵי לֵדָה, שְׁמוֹנָה יְמֵי מִילָה, שִׁבְעָה יְמֵי שַׁבַּתָּא, שִׁשָּׁה סִדְרֵי מִשְׁנָה, חֲמִשָּׁה חוּמְשֵׁי תוֹרָה, אַרְבַּע אִמָּהוֹת, שְׁלֹשָׁה אָבוֹת, שְׁנֵי לֻחוֹת הַבְּרִית, אֶחָד אֱלֹהֵינוּ שֶׁבַּשָּׁמַיִם וּבָאָרֶץ.

Who knows ten?
I know ten: ten are the
Ten Commandments; nine are
the months of pregnancy; eight
are the days until circumcision;
seven are the days of the week;
six are the Orders of Mishnah;
five are the Books of Torah; four
are the Matriarchs; three are the
Patriarchs; two are the Tablets;
one is our God,
in heaven and on earth.

עֲשָׂרָה מִי יוֹדֵעַ. עֲשָׂרָה אֲנִי יוֹדֵעַ: עֲשָׂרָה דִּבְּרַיָּא, תִּשְׁעָה יַרְחֵי לֵדָה, שְׁמוֹנָה יְמֵי מִילָה, שִׁבְעָה יְמֵי שַׁבַּתָּא, שִׁשָּׁה סִדְרֵי מִשְׁנָה, חֲמִשָּׁה חוּמְשֵׁי תוֹרָה, אַרְבַּע אִמָּהוֹת, שְׁלֹשָׁה אָבוֹת, שְׁנֵי לֻחוֹת הַבְּרִית, אֶחָד אֱלֹהֵינוּ שֶׁבַּשָּׁמַיִם וּבָאָרֶץ.

Who knows eleven?
I know eleven: eleven are the
stars (in Yosef's dream); ten are
the Ten Commandments; nine
are the months of pregnancy;
eight are the days until circumcision;
seven are the days of the week;
six are the Orders of Mishnah;
five are the Books of Torah; four
are the Matriarchs; three are the
Patriarchs; two are the Tablets;
one is our God,
in heaven and on earth.

Who knows twelve?
I know twelve: twelve are
the Tribes; eleven are the stars
(in Yosef's dream); ten are the
Ten Commandments; nine are
the months of pregnancy; eight
are the days until circumcision;
seven are the days of the week;
six are the Orders of Mishnah;
five are the Books of Torah; four
are the Matriarchs; three are the
Patriarchs; two are the Tablets;
one is our God,
in heaven and on earth.

אַחַד עָשָׂר מִי יוֹדֵעַ. אַחַד
עָשָׂר אֲנִי יוֹדֵעַ: אַחַד עָשָׂר
כּוֹכְבַיָּא, עֲשָׂרָה דִבְּרַיָּא, תִּשְׁעָה
יַרְחֵי לֵדָה, שְׁמוֹנָה יְמֵי מִילָה,
שִׁבְעָה יְמֵי שַׁבַּתָּא, שִׁשָּׁה סִדְרֵי
מִשְׁנָה, חֲמִשָּׁה חוּמְשֵׁי תוֹרָה,
אַרְבַּע אִמָּהוֹת, שְׁלֹשָׁה אָבוֹת,
שְׁנֵי לֻחוֹת הַבְּרִית, אֶחָד
אֱלֹהֵינוּ שֶׁבַּשָּׁמַיִם וּבָאָרֶץ.

שְׁנֵים עָשָׂר מִי יוֹדֵעַ. שְׁנֵים
עָשָׂר אֲנִי יוֹדֵעַ: שְׁנֵים עָשָׂר
שִׁבְטַיָּא, אַחַד עָשָׂר כּוֹכְבַיָּא,
עֲשָׂרָה דִבְּרַיָּא, תִּשְׁעָה יַרְחֵי
לֵדָה, שְׁמוֹנָה יְמֵי מִילָה, שִׁבְעָה
יְמֵי שַׁבַּתָּא, שִׁשָּׁה סִדְרֵי
מִשְׁנָה, חֲמִשָּׁה חוּמְשֵׁי תוֹרָה,
אַרְבַּע אִמָּהוֹת, שְׁלֹשָׁה אָבוֹת,
שְׁנֵי לֻחוֹת הַבְּרִית, אֶחָד
אֱלֹהֵינוּ שֶׁבַּשָּׁמַיִם וּבָאָרֶץ.

Who knows thirteen?
I know thirteen: thirteen are the
Attributes of Mercy; twelve are
the Tribes; eleven are the stars
(in Yosef's dream); ten are the
Ten Commandments; nine are
the months of pregnancy; eight
are the days until circumcision;
seven are the days of the week;
six are the Orders of Mishnah;
five are the Books of Torah; four
are the Matriarchs; three are the
Patriarchs; two are the Tablets;
one is our God,
in heaven and on earth.

שְׁלֹשָׁה עָשָׂר מִי יוֹדֵעַ.
שְׁלֹשָׁה עָשָׂר אֲנִי יוֹדֵעַ: שְׁלֹשָׁה
עָשָׂר מִדַּיָּא, שְׁנֵים עָשָׂר
שִׁבְטַיָּא, אַחַד עָשָׂר כּוֹכְבַיָּא,
עֲשָׂרָה דִבְּרַיָּא, תִּשְׁעָה יַרְחֵי
לֵדָה, שְׁמוֹנָה יְמֵי מִילָה, שִׁבְעָה
יְמֵי שַׁבַּתָּא, שִׁשָּׁה סִדְרֵי
מִשְׁנָה, חֲמִשָּׁה חוּמְשֵׁי תוֹרָה,
אַרְבַּע אִמָּהוֹת, שְׁלֹשָׁה אָבוֹת,
שְׁנֵי לֻחוֹת הַבְּרִית, אֶחָד
אֱלֹהֵינוּ שֶׁבַּשָּׁמַיִם וּבָאָרֶץ.

חַד גַּדְיָא, חַד גַּדְיָא דְזַבִּין אַבָּא
בִּתְרֵי זוּזֵי, חַד גַּדְיָא, חַד גַּדְיָא.

וְאָתָא שׁוּנְרָא, וְאָכְלָה לְגַדְיָא, דְזַבִּין
אַבָּא בִּתְרֵי זוּזֵי, חַד גַּדְיָא, חַד גַּדְיָא.

וְאָתָא כַלְבָּא, וְנָשַׁךְ לְשׁוּנְרָא,
דְאָכְלָה לְגַדְיָא, דְזַבִּין אַבָּא בִּתְרֵי
זוּזֵי, חַד גַּדְיָא, חַד גַּדְיָא.

וְאָתָא חוּטְרָא, וְהִכָּה לְכַלְבָּא,
דְנָשַׁךְ לְשׁוּנְרָא, דְאָכְלָה לְגַדְיָא,
דְזַבִּין אַבָּא בִּתְרֵי זוּזֵי, חַד גַּדְיָא,
חַד גַּדְיָא.

וְאָתָא נוּרָא, וְשָׂרַף לְחוּטְרָא, דְהִכָּה
לְכַלְבָּא, דְנָשַׁךְ לְשׁוּנְרָא, דְאָכְלָה
לְגַדְיָא, דְזַבִּין אַבָּא בִּתְרֵי זוּזֵי, חַד
גַּדְיָא, חַד גַּדְיָא.

וְאָתָא מַיָּא, וְכָבָה לְנוּרָא, דְשָׂרַף
לְחוּטְרָא, דְהִכָּה לְכַלְבָּא, דְנָשַׁךְ
לְשׁוּנְרָא, דְאָכְלָה לְגַדְיָא, דְזַבִּין
אַבָּא בִּתְרֵי זוּזֵי, חַד גַּדְיָא, חַד גַּדְיָא.

וְאָתָא תוֹרָא, וְשָׁתָא לְמַיָּא, דְכָבָה
לְנוּרָא, דְשָׂרַף לְחוּטְרָא, דְהִכָּה
לְכַלְבָּא, דְנָשַׁךְ לְשׁוּנְרָא, דְאָכְלָה
לְגַדְיָא, דְזַבִּין אַבָּא בִּתְרֵי זוּזֵי, חַד
גַּדְיָא, חַד גַּדְיָא.

Had Gadya

One kid, one kid,
that father bought for two zuzim,
one kid, one kid.

Along came a cat and ate the kid,
that father bought for two zuzim,
one kid, one kid.

Along came a dog and bit
the cat, that ate the kid,
that father bought for two zuzim,
one kid, one kid.

Along came a stick and beat the dog,
that bit the cat, that ate the kid,
that father bought for two zuzim,
one kid, one kid.

Along came a fire and burned the stick,
that beat the dog, that bit
the cat, that ate the kid,
that father bought for two zuzim,
one kid, one kid.

Along came water and extinguished
the fire, that burned the stick,
that beat the dog, that bit
the cat, that ate the kid,
that father bought for two zuzim,
one kid, one kid.

Along came an ox and drank the water,
that extinguished the fire,
that burned the stick, that beat the dog,
that bit the cat, that ate the kid,
that father bought for two zuzim,
one kid, one kid.

Along came a slaughterer and
slaughtered the ox, that drank
the water, that extinguished
the fire, that burned the stick,
that beat the dog, that bit
the cat, that ate the kid,
that father bought for two zuzim,
one kid, one kid.

וְאָתָא הַשׁוֹחֵט, וְשָׁחַט לְתוֹרָא,
דְּשָׁתָא לְמַיָּא, דְּכָבָה לְנוּרָא, דְּשָׂרַף
לְחוּטְרָא,דְּהִכָּה לְכַלְבָּא, דְּנָשַׁךְ
לְשׁוּנְרָא, דְּאָכְלָה לְגַדְיָא, דְזַבִּין
אַבָּא בִּתְרֵי זוּזֵי, חַד גַּדְיָא, חַד גַּדְיָא.

Along came the Angel of Death
and killed the slaughterer, who
slaughtered the ox, that drank
the water, that extinguished
the fire, that burned the stick,
that beat the dog, that bit
the cat, that ate the kid,
that father bought for two zuzim,
one kid, one kid.

וְאָתָא מַלְאַךְ הַמָּוֶת, וְשָׁחַט לְשׁוֹחֵט,
דְּשָׁחַט לְתוֹרָא, דְּשָׁתָא לְמַיָּא,
דְּכָבָה לְנוּרָא, דְּשָׂרַף
לְחוּטְרָא,דְּהִכָּה לְכַלְבָּא, דְּנָשַׁךְ
לְשׁוּנְרָא, דְּאָכְלָה לְגַדְיָא, דְזַבִּין
אַבָּא בִּתְרֵי זוּזֵי, חַד גַּדְיָא, חַד גַּדְיָא.

Then the Holy One, blessed
is He, came and slew the Angel
of Death, who killed the
slaughterer, who slaughtered
the ox, that drank the water,
that extinguished the fire,
that burned the stick,
that beat the dog, that bit
the cat, that ate the kid,
that father bought for two zuzim,
one kid, one kid.

וְאָתָא הַקָּדוֹשׁ בָּרוּךְ הוּא, וְשָׁחַט
לְמַלְאַךְ הַמָּוֶת, דְּשָׁחַט לְתוֹרָא,
דְּשָׁתָא לְמַיָּא, דְּכָבָה לְנוּרָא, דְּשָׂרַף
לְחוּטְרָא, דְּהִכָּה לְכַלְבָּא, דְּנָשַׁךְ
לְשׁוּנְרָא, דְּאָכְלָה לְגַדְיָא, דְזַבִּין
אַבָּא בִּתְרֵי זוּזֵי, חַד גַּדְיָא, חַד גַּדְיָא.

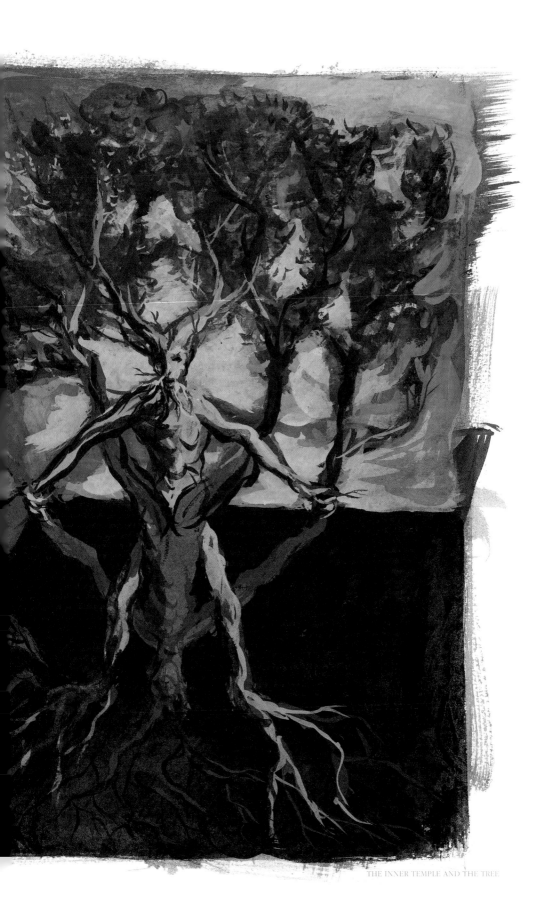

NIRTZAH

ending of the ceremony

REMEMBER YOUR FUTURE

The word "nirtzah" is difficult to translate. Derived from the root "ratzo," it means "to be wanted," "desired." Now that we have completed the Seder according to the prescriptions, we are called by the Creator and invited into the upper worlds. We open ourselves up to the future and to a true self-transformation. After the Liberation lived in the reciting of the Haggadah, after the mystical Revelation that we can feel in silent meditation and in greeting Elijah the prophet, we live a time of Redemption.

The last part of the Haggadah consists of songs, and on the second Seder night (in the Diaspora) in the counting of the Omer.

The period between Pesach and Shavuoth (the Feast of Weeks) is called the Omer. It lasts forty-nine days. The word "Omer" designates a measure of capacity, approximately four liters, used during biblical times. However, this word has other meanings. It refers to the counting of forty-nine days, seven weeks, because, while the Temple stood, every day, beginning on the second day of the Passover festival, an omer of barley, the first harvest of the season. was offered there. Now, in memory of the Omer offered in the Temple, Jews recite the benediction for counting the Omer every night between Passover and Shavuoth, and they then count the number of days and weeks. For example, on the last evening, we say: "today is the forty-ninth day, which is seven weeks of the Omer."

The purpose of this counting is to become aware of the necessary progression between liberation and revelation. Every day must be the time of a new experience. We must open ourselves to time and to the plans for the future. To finish the Seder is to be filled with so much energy that we are already making plans. This orientation toward the future is expressed in the fact that all the songs that we sing in this part of the Seder move from the few to the many: always higher, always farther.

Here we find the sense of the Hebraic ethic: to be directed toward the future, toward the achievement of the project of nirtzah, which is the dimension of "forward," of "before me," "of projection toward the forward part of my being, the dimension of the living, inner force that dwells within me, of my inner destination."

In Hebrew, the word "living" is "chay" (written with two letters in Hebrew). The word for "what is living over there" is "sham chay," written with four letters, and the same four Hebrew letters, transposed, spell the word "mashiach," the "messiah." The possibility that there is something beyond the present and beyond the self is none other than the dimension of the messiah: messianic time. As Rabbi Nachman of Bratslav said, "It is forbidden to despair," because there is always, just a bit further, a door that will open to the future!

Here again, the end of the Haggadah comes back to its beginning, the sanctification of time, or the kiddush, which we have explained as the obligation to leave behind banality. We must transform the night of Passover into a challenge: to experience our originality and our. Messianism, that is, our capacity to invent ourselves and project ourselves into the future, cannot be achieved without us. The messiah is us, each of us. "Remember your future," says Rabbi Nachman. That is to say, "Don't forget your responsibility in the creation of your own future."

"Then one understands," says Martin Buber, "that every person born in this world represents something new, something that did not exist before, something original and unique."

All Jewish people have the duty of appreciating that they are unique in this world, by their own particular character, and that there has never been anyone else like them. For if there had already been someone like them, there would be no reason for them to be in this world.

All human beings, individually, are new creatures in the world, and they are called upon to fulfill their particularity in this world. The very first task of every person is the actualization of their unique possibilities, without precedent, and always renewed—and not the repetition of something that someone else, not even the greatest of people, has already done. This is the idea expressed by Rabbi Zushe shortly before his death: "In the world to come, they won't ask me, 'why weren't you Moses?' They will ask me, 'Why weren't you Zushe?'"

Why haven't you been yourself?

THE THREE MATZOT

THE MANNA

(EXODUS 16:15)

THE DISCIPLE AND THE MASTER

GOD'S HAND

PSALMS 118

PURIFICATION OF THE HANDS

THE MAROR

THE WINE AND THE SECRET

(JEREMIAH 25:15)

THE MEAL

(ECCLESIASTES 3:1)

THE MAROR

THE SEVEN LADDERS

WITH SEVEN RUNGS

THE MIDDLE OF THE NIGHT

(GENESIS 14:14)

THE ORCHARD

LISTENING AND THE LAW

"HERE IT IS"

THE SEDER PLATE AND
THE ORDER OF THE SEFIROT

THE EYE

THE CREATION OF THE WORLD
AND THE SEFIROT

LISTENING AND WAITING

JOSEPH IN THE PIT
(GENESIS 37:22)

THE PEOPLE
AND THE SEA

THE CONSTRUCTION
OF TIME AND PLACE

AT NIGHT

THE FIVE MASTERS
OF THE LAW

EXODUS 12:34

A DEEP SLEEP FELL
UPON ABRAHAM (GENESIS 15:12)

THE FIFTEEN STEPS
OF THE HOLY TEMPLE

THE PEOPLE CROSS THE RED SEA

JOSEPH'S SECOND DREAM
(GENESIS 37:9)

AFIKOMAN

THE AFIKOMAN GAME

JACOB'S DREAM

(GENESIS 28:12)

THE SONG

GENESIS 31:45

THE NIGHT OF THE TENT

(GENESIS 15:15)

THE GOLD

AND THE SILVER

THE ANGEL OF DEATH

(EXODUS 12:12)

THE PROPHET ELIJAH AND THE REVELATION

(1 KINGS 19:2)

THE GIVING OF THE LAW

THE INNER TEMPLE AND THE TREE

THE EMPTY CHAIR

AND ELIJAH'S CUP

Gérard Garouste wishes to thank Elisabeth Garouste, Henri Berestychi, François Rachline and Yakov Aaroch.

The idea of writing a commentary on the Haggadah has fascinated me, one might say, since I was a boy. I have marvelous memories of being a child at the immense table where many guests are assembled, in particular my great-uncle Fernand Ehrlich and his wife Reine, in the place of the Elders. I see my father, then and now, trying to present commentaries that have never before been given, yet finally going back to the commentaries of Dr. Robert Nerson's Haggadah. The present Haggadah is to some degree a homage to Nerson's Haggadah, which is connected to so many wonderful memories of this holiday and of spring, when one feels the world in its freshness and new beginnings. Since then my father has written his own Haggadah in his book, From Generation to Generation. *Nevertheless, every year he takes up Nerson's Haggadah again, almost like a ritual.*

When I began to write a commentary on the Haggadah, I did not hesitate for a moment regarding the choice of the text and the commentaries which would provide the primary reference point for me: the Haggadah of Dr. Nerson. Thus the reader should not be surprised to find in these thoughts both of the spirit of the traditional commentaries of Nerson's Haggadah (which itself followed in the footsteps of the Haggadot of Edmond Fleg and Joseph Bloch), and also the main lines of the teachings of my father, Rabbi Jacques Ouaknin, as well as the pedagogical enthusiasm of my mother, Eliane-Sophie Ouaknin. May both of them find here the expression of my gratitude!

We also thank warmly Librairie Colbo for graciously permitting us to use the translation of Nerson's Haggadah, of which they were the first publishers.

A book is a great adventure. It is always a perfect occasion for gatherings, discussions, and challenges, both intellectual and technical. More than in my earlier books, I wish to express here my thanks and my debt toward all those who have made possible the birth of this magnificent volume.

First of all, I would like to thank Gérard Garouste for agreeing to collaborate on such a project. More than two years ago, when I first visited him to propose that we work together on this Haggadah, he agreed with enthusiasm and set to work immediately, giving, I believe, the best of himself with utmost generosity. After a preliminary reading and interpretation of the Haggadah, Gérard Garouste produced a series of extraordinary and magnificent paintings, to which he later added other works, just as impressive, inspired by my own commentaries on the Haggadah and the dialogue that we held concerning this book. May he find here the expression both of my deep and warm friendship and also of my highest admiration.

The complexity of creating a layout for this book—which consists of English text backed by a commentary and also a Hebrew text composed of several levels, as well as illustrations of many dimensions, colors, and mediums—has necessitated close collaboration among several book designers.

I also wish to express particular thanks to Mathilde Dupuy d'Angeac, who, with patience and talent, devoted several months to resolving the difficult technical problems of designing this book.

It would have been impossible to create this book without the precious and effective collaboration of Bertrand Laidain, who designed and produced the Hebrew text and inserted it into the labyrinth of the text and the illustrations by Garouste. I am grateful for the effort, patience, and skill that he showed in completing this meticulous and magnificent work.

I also wish to thank my friend Frank Lalou, who helped us find a solution for producing the Hebrew text. Thanks for his indefatigable generosity.

I received extremely valuable assistance from my friend and colleague, Rabbi Pierre-Yves Bauer, who spent many hours reading the text meticulously to avoid possible errors regarding the meaning of the words, the translation, and the commentaries, as well as the logic and coherence of the connection between the Hebrew and the original French text, that was then translated into English. I would like to express my deepest friendship and gratitude for his precious collaboration.

I also wish to thank Laurence Sigal, the curator of the Museum of Jewish Art in Paris, who exhibited the original artwork created by Gérard Garouste for this book.

I would also like to express warm thanks to Julie David, who supervised this project with great seriousness and efficiency, and who managed to harmonize the text and the schedules of those involved so that the book would be as close to perfection as possible.

The English translation of this book was done by Jeffrey Green, who thus endowed it with wings to cross the Atlantic. May he find here the expression of my warm friendship!

The English version would not have seen the light of day without the diligence and supervision of the dynamic team of Assouline Publishing in New York, especially Dorothée Walliser and Marissa Pelton, whom I wish to thank particularly.

As with each of my earlier works, the written version follows an oral version that I presented in the framework of various courses and lectures. Here I would like to take the opportunity to thank the institutions and individuals whose guest I was: Monique Sander (Centre Aleph), Helene Attali (the friends of Aliyah and of the Rue Copernic Synagogue), Lazare and Laurence Kaplan, who continue to practice with discretion and talent the art of welcoming people in which the late and regretted Mary Kaplan so distinguished herself. May both of them find here the expression of my gratitude and deepest friendship.

Finally I would also like to express friendship and gratitude to Martine Assouline, who, as usual, has achieved the miracle of publishing a book, combining technical prowess with the more complex ability of understanding the psychology of an author and a team.

Let no one think that I have forgotten Prosper Assouline, whose artistic inspiration and great talent regarding the meaning of books is present on every page. Thank you one and all!

Marc-Alain Ouaknin

The following edition of the Haggadah,
with commentary by Marc-Alain Ouaknin,
illustrated by Gérard Garouste,
was printed by Pizzi in Milan (Italy).
The illustrations were color separated
by Gravor in Brügg (Switzerland).
One thousand and seven hundred copies
were printed on Acquarello paper,
in a cloth-covered box,
and are the original editions in English.

February 2001